Observation and Explanation:

A Guide to Philosophy of Science

HARPER ESSAYS IN PHILOSOPHY

Edited by Arthur C. Danto

Arthur C. Danto	WHAT PHILOSOPHY IS
Norwood Russell Hanson	OBSERVATION AND EXPLANATION: A GUIDE TO PHILOSOPHY OF SCIENCE
Jerrold J. Katz	THE UNDERLYING REALITY OF LANGUAGE AND ITS PHILOSOPHICAL IMPORT
Norman Malcolm	PROBLEMS OF MIND
David Pears	WHAT IS KNOWLEDGE?
Hilary Putnam	PHILOSOPHY OF LOGIC
B. A. O. Williams	MORAL PHILOSOPHY
Robert Paul Wolff	IN DEFENSE OF ANARCHISM
Richard Wollheim	ART AND ITS OBJECTS

Observation and Explanation:

A Guide to Philosophy of Science

———◆—◆—◆———

by Norwood Russell Hanson

Preface by
Stephen Toulmin

A TORCHBOOK LIBRARY EDITION
Harper & Row, Publishers
New York, Evanston, San Francisco, London

OBSERVATION AND EXPLANATION: A GUIDE TO PHILOSOPHY OF SCIENCE

copyright © 1971 by F. Fay Hanson.
Introduction copyright © 1971 by Stephen Toulmin.

First HARPER TORCHBOOK EDITION published 1971.

STANDARD BOOK NUMBER (cloth): 06–136046–5

LIBRARY OF CONGRESS CATALOG CARD NUMBER: 76–154654

Contents

Preface	vii
Observation	1
Facts	9
Measurement	16
Induction	19
Experiment	23
Causality	28
Explanation	39
Theories	45
Laws	49
Hypothetico-Deduction	60
Retroduction	63
Theoretical Entities	68
Craig's Theorem	69
Verification	73
Falsification	76
Models	77

Preface

———◆◆◆———

Norwood Russell Hanson (1924–67) was a man out
of his time, a character from the Florentine Renais-
sance growing up in the contemporary United States.
Hanson showed how much can still be achieved, even
within the professionalized technocratic society of
the mid-twentieth century, by the true *amateur:* the
man who makes himself the master of an art or science out of curiosity, love or sheer cussedness, quite
unconnected with the business of earning a living.
And he showed how such an amateur can achieve a
kind of richness and variety of experience in a whole
range of activities which spills over the boundaries
between them. In this way, he became a "jack of
many trades" and, in his own very special way, a
master of them all.

When Russ Hanson died in April 1967, he was
piloting his own personal Grumman Bearcat, in
which he had been planning to attack the world air-
speed record for piston-engined planes. (He had
learned to fly as a U.S. Navy pilot during World
War II and, during his years at Yale, he would give

summer aerobatic displays under the soubriquet of "The Flying Professor.") But he was also a talented musician, improvising at the organ or on the horn or trumpet, and equally a remarkable draftsman, with a special flair for grotesque and imaginative figure drawings reminiscent of Fuseli or Blake. If his own house needed attention, again, he would do the work himself; manhandling steel girders into position which many builders would have blanched at. Even the theoretical physics which he wrote about so authoritatively and confidently as a philosopher was largely self-taught; and, by the last years of his life, he could discuss the most technical problems of quantum mechanics with leading professionals in the field, in a way that won their respect—in strange contrast to the frustrated exasperation with which working scientists regard the arguments of most professional philosophers of science.

Hanson got his university education largely as a returned serviceman, at Chicago and Columbia Universities, and he went on as a graduate to Oxford. There he quickly added a mastery of the methods of post-war British philosophical analysis to his earlier skills, and was appointed to a University Lecturership in Philosophy of Science at Cambridge University. After the Suez affair of 1956, disillusioned with Britain, he moved back to his native U.S.A. and threw himself into the task of organizing the newly-created interdisciplinary department for the History and Philosophy of Science at Indiana University, which owes its continuing impetus largely to his efforts.

Hanson's essays and polemical writings cover the whole spectrum from philosophical logic to theology —the theology, needless to say, of an unbeliever; for in religion, as in all things, he was strongly counter-suggestible. Dogmatism, even in defense of views he happened to support, would rouse his disputatiousness; worse still than believing "the right thing for the wrong reason," was believing anything for no particular reason at all. The two books published in his lifetime, on *Patterns of Discovery* and *The Concept of the Positron,* were both of them intellectual plum-cakes; variable in texture, but stuffed with good things. The essay which follows gives us more characteristic snatches of that flavory, idiomatic style, which he made so much his own and which his friends came so much to appreciate.

STEPHEN TOULMIN
January 1971

Observation

Pascal placed man midway between the angels and the brutes. It is from this positioning, he felt, that the 'human predicament' arises. Science, the glorious achievement of modern man, is itself analogously situated between pure mathematics and raw sense experience; it is from the conceptual tension generated between these polar coordinates that *philosophical* perplexities about science arise.

This is the format of all that follows. Our 'Guide to Philosophy of Science' will course through a conceptual terrain of standard issues—focusing first on the Scylla of formalism, and then sighting on the Charybdis of sensationalism. Most philosophical discussions of science move initially toward the bare, jagged rocks of symbology, and then back toward the other extreme—the turbulent, teeming maelstrom of phenomenology. Frightening formalism to starboard; formless empiricism to port! The most fruitful of these *engagements du voyage* resist toppling toward either disaster, steering rather along the thin line of balanced reason and cautious moderation faintly discernible between.

Our strategy here will be to delineate these ex-
tremes (of 'sensationalistic thesis' and 'formalistic
antithesis'), noting some of their attractions and
their disadvantages. A balanced 'middle of the
channel' resolution (a 'stable and realistic synthesis'), will be the objective sought at each stage in
the winding journey which we now begin.

Natural science is concerned with the facts of this
world. The results of that concern are articulated in
factual statements. (No collection of *non*factual
statements could ever constitute a natural science.)
But factual statements have this property: they are
'synthetic' vis-à-vis their sign-design. That is, every
factual statement is such that its denial does *not*
generate any formal inconsistency. S is synthetic
(within a language L), if and only if it is consistent
while not-S is also consistent; neither S, nor not-S,
generates (in L) anything of the form Q *and not-Q*.
Such an S could be a factual statement in L just because the question "Is S a statement of fact?" cannot be answered through analysis alone.

How then can one determine of any given factual
statement S whether or not it is true—i.e., a statement of fact? Semantical and symbolical scrutiny is
not enough; nothing by way of syntax study, or of
meaning analysis, can single out via inspection alone
some one S as acceptable, while not-S is discarded.
This, because both S and not-S are logically consistent—which is just to say again that S, since it is a
factual statement, is synthetic.

Observational experience is required to screen
those factual statements which 'obtain' from those

which do not—the former alone being candidates for inclusion within systems of informative natural science. (No collection of factual statements known to be *false* could ever constitute a natural science.)

But this makes the process of observation sound somewhat 'Pavlovian', does it not? It suggests that factual statements come in pairs (S and not-S), then to be 'subjected' to observational testing ('ding-a-ling'), so that either S or not-S will emerge corroborated (salivation!). It suggests something like 'acid' or 'base' being indicated as the response of a litmus test-paper thrust into some liquid. What is it about scientific observations which corresponds to such a litmus paper reaction? Where, and when, does data-registration *simpliciter* dominate? (How passive can an observational determination of truth or falsity get?)

Granted, in experimental situations involving titrations, or litmus paper reactions, or salivation in response to a bell-ring, the observer's sensation-report *may* be a datum of significance. 'Red now' or 'ding-a-ling' may be observation-signals of primary importance in such contexts. The tastes of acids, the odors of gases, the textures of surfaces, the colors of fluids, the warmth of circuits, etc.—these all require normal observers, with standard sense-neuro-circuitry, in order to determine which factual claims are true, and which ones false. 'The observer' in these cases is no more than an animated detector; depersonalized, he is just a reticulum of signal receivers integrated with considerable mechanical efficiency and reliability. To this extent and on this account, *any* normal person could make scientifically valuable observations. The color-blind chemist needs help from someone with normal vision to complete his titration work—whether this someone be another chemist, or his six-year-old son, does not matter. But, now, are there any observations that the latter, the child, could *not* make?

Consider the following passage written by Pierre Duhem:

> Enter a laboratory; approach the table crowded with an assortment of apparatus, an electric cell, silk-covered copper wire, small cups of Mercury, spools, a mirror mounted on an iron bar; the experimenter is inserting into small openings the metal ends of ebony-headed pins; the iron bar oscillates, and the mirror attached to it throws a luminous band upon a celluloid scale; the forward-backward motion of this spot enables the physicist to observe the minute oscillations of the iron bar. But ask him what he is doing. Will he answer 'I am studying the oscillations of an iron bar which carries a mirror'? No, he will say that he is measuring the electrical resistance of the spools. If you are astonished, if you ask him what his words mean, what relation they have with the phenomenon he has been observing and which you have noted at the same time as he, he will answer that your question requires a long explanation and that you should take a course in electricity.—*La Théorie Physique* (Paris, 1914), p. 218.

Thus, to observe what Duhem's physicist takes himself to be observing requires somewhat more than normal vision. Optical signal-receptors, however sensitive and acute, cannot provide everything needed for observing electrical resistance. *Knowledge* is also presupposed; scientific observation is thus a 'theory-laden' activity (to use an expression, from *Patterns of Discovery*,* which seems now to be in vogue). Brainless, photosensitive computers—infants and squirrels too—do not make scientific observations, however remarkable their signal-reception and storage may be. This can be no surprise to any reader of this book. That the motion of Mars is retrograde, that a fluid's flow is laminar, that a plane's wing-skin friction increases rapidly with descent, that there is a calcium deficiency in Connecticut soil, that the North American water table has dropped—these all concern observations which by far exceed the order of sophistication possible through raw sense experience. Nor are these cases of simply requiring physicobiological 'extensions' to the senses we already have; for telescopes, microscopes, heat sensors, etc., are not sufficient to determine that Mars's motion is retrograde, that blood poisoning is setting in, that volcanic activity is immanent. Being able to make sense of the sensors requires knowledge and theory—not simply more sense signals. (Understanding the significance of the signal flags fluttering from the bridge of the *Queen Elizabeth* does not usually require still *more* flags to be flown!)

This recognition of a strong theoretical element

---

* Norwood R. Hanson, *Patterns of Discovery: An Enquiry into the Conceptual Foundations of Science* (New York: Cambridge U. Press, 1968).

within scientific observation sometimes drives philosophers to hint that the incoming signals from 'the subject matter' are less important than they really are. For a Descartes, a Poincaré, or an Eddington, observation can shrink to being little more than the provision of values for variables in a theoretical algorithm—in a framework of 'understanding'. Laboratory instruments, measurement, and experimental design, for such thinkers, may seem geared only to the supplying of 'initial conditions'—the barest localized starting points for scientific reflection. Such conditions only resemble 'the given' within mathematical computation, the *occasion* for problems, not their solutions—not 'knowledge' properly so-called. Even as such, they must often be 'corrected', reshaped and processed for further usefulness within a computational system. The theorist presses observers with challenges like "To what degree are departures from the 'ideal case' attributable merely to the crudeness of the experimental apparatus?", "How fundamental to our *understanding* of phenomena are your detected deflections, error-spreads, frictions, dislocations, deformations, etc.—all things inseparable from your instruments and techniques of measurement?" "In short, where can we ignore the 'side effects' of the insufficiently sensitive probes you use (and which, alas, hold our attention) and ponder instead the *essential* aspects of the events themselves?"

Here, it is as if the 'conceptual shape' of one's theories, the posture and stature of one's presuppositions, determine where observations have to be 'cleaned up'—where they should be realigned and reprocessed effectively to be plugged into a science's theoretical framework, its structure for intelligibility.

Doubtless, recognizing this central feature of scientific observation is very important. Understanding of actual phenomena is often advanced by studies of ideal fluids, frictionless surfaces, strictly rigid levers, perfectly elastic bodies, infinite wing spans, one-dimensional translations, point particles, and 'pure cases' generally. When our ideas of processes are structured by such crisp conceptions, the thousand natural shocks of actual observation can be smoothed and made tractable in terms of 'what is reasonable'. Inexpert plumbing, bad carpentry, and poor laboratory-bench technique need not shape our comprehension of a science's subject matter. This attitude was well conveyed by Laplace when he wrote:

> Astronomy is a great problem of mechanics in which the elements of the motions are the arbitrary constant quantities. The solution depends upon the accuracy of the observations, and upon the perfection of the analysis. It is very important to reject every empirical process, and to complete the analysis, *so that it shall not be necessary to derive from observation any but indispensable data.—Mécanique Céleste* (1799–1825), vol. 1.

Athough Laplace recognized the indispensability of observation at *some* point (if ever scientific theory is to be harnessed to the natural world 'outside'), it was yet his wish to keep the observational-descriptive content of analytical science down to the barest minimum. Thus the major function of the scientific enterprise—to wit, the attainment of theoretical understanding, of knowledge—should be hampered as little as possible by laboratory 'busywork'. Refinements in conduitry and circuitry, in beam-focusing and detector-positioning, in spectrometry, thermometry, and hydrometry—these may lead to more decimal places as one reports the results of measurements, but they rarely determine a new *form* for an equation, or a new kind of *inference* concerning an old subject matter.

Periodically, however, theoreticians get caught up in a 'so-much-the-worse-for-the facts' attitude. Historically, such confidence almost appears to be understandable—especially in the wake of 'discoveries required by theory' such as those of the antiproton, the antineutron, the neutrino, Anderson's positron, the planet Neptune (whose discoverer was Leverrier the theoretician; not d'Arret, Galle's assistant, the first man whose retina distinguished that new light-point), etc. But still, the philosophical 'middle way' must always be the one which recognizes *significant* observations within a science as those which at once meet the criteria of relevance embodied within extant theory, while also being capable of *modifying* that theory by the hard, stubborn recognition of 'what is the case', of *the facts*. Science does not make the facts, however much it may shape, color, and sort them!

Facts

Observations are *of* such things as particle-pairs, perturbations, and pollination. Facts are *that* (or to the effect that), for example, pair production occurred in a cosmic ray shower at *x, y, z* and *t.* Another fact is that our moon perturbs, or deflects, artificial satellites from their 'pure' (Keplerian) circumterrestrial orbits. Still another fact is to the effect that our sun is located 30,000 light-years from the center of our galaxy.

'That'-clause linguistic constructions are always close to any articulation of what the facts are— necessarily so. This should suggest some conceptual intimacy between what we count as facts and the language we state them in—or at least between the facts and the types of logical entity we designate as 'statements'. Statement *S* states *that x, y,* and *z.* If *S* is true, then *the fact* must be that *x, y, z.* Such a verification may have proceeded via a scientist's observation *of* whatever was described truly by *S.* (The conceptual lines are not sharp here, of course; the scientist might be said to have observed *that x, y, z,* thereby rendering the truth of *S* perspicuous. But the trend seems clear.) Our observations of, for example, flowers and bees, and what they do (*S*) may establish it for us as a fact *that S,* in which case —should we choose to express ourselves linguistically to that effect—we shall state *that S.* We observe objects, processes, and events. But facts must be a different kind of denotatum, logically different. We

do not observe facts (what would they look like?).
Facts are not objects or collections of objects or con-
stellations of objects. Facts are *to the effect that,*
e.g., a bee, while sipping a flower's nectar, gathers
pollen on its limbs, later deposits it on other plants,
thereby fertilizing them. A statement to that effect
would be true, or false, in virtue of facts of this
type—and not because of the simple existence of
bees and flowers, and certainly not because such
facts *are* bees and flowers, or their geometrical interrelationships, or true statements about them.
Facts are what true statements state.

Attempts to construe facts as objects, or constella-
tions of objects, have been notorious during this
century. The motivation is always the same; if color-
terms are to be directly correlated with colors, and
names directly correlated with objects, then statements (presumably) are directly to be related with
facts—such as might be photographed, transported,
or boxed—just as with any arrangement of objects
and processes. 'Red' links with the poppy's color;
'Fido' links with that kennel's occupant; so, also,
what is expressed 'Fido's tongue is red' links with
Fido's tongue as it is colored—i.e., the fact that
Fido's tongue is red. The statement describes the
tongue, states a fact about it. *Ergo* the fact is the
red tongue—so slides the slippery argument. But
the notions of photographing facts (red tongues?),
of transporting what true statements state, of fenc-
ing in, or wrapping, what experiment and observation reveals to be the case (can we box the fact that
Fido's tongue is red?)—something goes awry with

such notions and with these ways of expressing
them. We state facts, we list them, we file them for
further reference. Object-clusters do not accommodate to such locutions. (We cannot state Fido.) Still,
it is the hard, stubborn, objective, and intractable
feature of 'the facts'—which *are what they are* ir-
respective of anyone's pet theories to the contrary—
it is this that has drawn some philosophical worthies
toward the position that facts are but another kind
of furniture within the warehouse of the world.
(Bertrand Russell's *Logical Atomism* lectures are a
case in point.) In principle they are no different, for
such philosophers, from object-clusters, event-con-
stellations, and configurations of situations—all
these being photographable, enclosable, datable de-
nota, which facts are not. To this way of thinking,
then, the *direct* outcome of experimentation, observation, testing, and measurement is, and always has
been, the facts—the objects, events, and situations
exposed on the bench, at the observatory, in the field.

Noting the conceptual intimacy which obtains between 'the facts' and statements of the facts, however, suggests to other philosophers that there can
be nothing logically less complicated about facts than
about statements themselves. Since statements are
conceptually more intricate than names, so also facts
must be conceptually more intricate than objects;
more intricate than object-clusters too. The theory-
laden character of 'the facts' soon comes to impress
such thinkers even more forcibly than is the case
with observation. For whatever it is 'out there' that
makes us say (truly) that the space immediately ad-

jacent to our sun is non-Euclidean, or that the symmetry properties obtaining within our universe indicate the existence of an antiparticle corresponding to each kind of 'familiar' particle now known —these 'whatevers' must count as *facts*. Such 'whatevers' are accorded 'fact-hood' because they 'anchor' the least vulnerable statements within extant theoretical physics. The philosophical tendency here, then, will be to construe 'the facts' as those objective organizations of the objects, events, and states of affairs within a scientific subject matter which render true the theories we do hold. The view thus arises that 'the facts' are just those conditions a subject matter meets such that a given theory might be applied to it—the boundary conditions. In that sense the facts are 'theoretically determined'— somewhat as the rules of chess determine what layout the chessboard must have at the onset, and what moves will be permissible therefrom so that the subsequent interchange could be describable as 'chess'. Thus, in a Wittgensteinian view:

> . . . the fact that it can be described by Newtonian mechanics asserts nothing about the world; but *this* asserts something, namely, that it can be described in that particular way in which as a matter of fact it is described.—*Tractatus Logico-Philosophicus* (London, 1922), b.342.

'Possible science' is thus a potential infinitude of possible theories—scientific idea-games—some of which will apply to *de facto* subject matters, but most of which will not. Applicable or not, such concept-networks are identifiable statement-structures, as were the phlogiston and caloric theories. *The facts,* on this breathtaking view, are just those objective, 3-D conditions a subject matter must meet in order to qualify as tractable and intelligible through the lenses of *this* theory, or *that* one, or *those;* and in some cases, of course, 'the phenomenal facts' meet the boundary conditions of no extant theory whatever (e.g., inversion layers in ancient Greece, lodestone-magnetism for Charlemagne, firefly luminescence in Galileo's day, ESP today). Then, the subject matter in question is (temporarily, it is always hoped) 'beyond science'. With respect to such complexes of phenomena, considerable confusion concerning what *are* the facts always abounds.

Here once again we see philosophical attitudes (now those concerning *facts*) ranging all the way from brute empiricism to an almost abstract theoretical idealism. But here, as everywhere in the philosophical firmament, there is a *via media.*

Note a conceptual feature of *scenes* and *landscapes.* As a skilled artist confronts the scene at dawn he may be moved to convey those colors, shapes, and textures to canvas. After his having done so, we may remark the likeness between the scene 'out there' (to the east) and the scene we view on his canvas. He is indeed a skilled *landscape* painter! As the landscape gardener works through the actual trees and shrubs on the eastern slopes, so our artist 'works through' the corresponding patches on his canvas. The landscape is 'out there'; but it is also captured forever in his painting. 'Scene' and 'landscape' are thus Janus-faced terms. The complex of 3-D objects to the east at dawn is such that it *can* be captured on canvas: it is that *kind* of designatum. The scenes continually before our eyes comprise the *possibilities* inherent in objects and events *to be* captured on canvas, or to be fixed in photographs. The painting (if it makes a successful 'capture') will be 'true to life'. *The same scene* is thus apprehendable in several ways—'out there' *in rerum natura,* and as on canvas, in home movies, in mirrors, etc.

The analogy with *facts* should be quite apparent. The possibilities of their being described in this way, or in that way, constitute objective features of events and processes in our world. To the extent that our descriptions (rendered more articulate and precise through algebra) instantiate such possibilities—to that same extent they are *true.*

The scientific description is true, then, when it states 'the facts'. And again, what are 'the facts'? Just those *structural* possibilities inherent within states of affairs such that some statements made about these states will be certifiably true, and some will be certifiably false. *What* the statements *state* when they are true (and, of course, what they deny when they are false)—these are the facts. The facts, then, constitute true-statement-possibilities ('describabilia') within the subject matter. 'Fact' is also a Janus-faced term, then. The facts are 'out there' in the subject matter—'there' and potentially describable even before anyone has articulated them. Yet, once embodied within a language, those same facts are *stated,* i.e., expressed explicity. Facts are 'out there', yet statable. Facts, then, are the *describabilia* of this world. Before being captured by language they are 'natural *describabilia';* after language-capture they are 'expressed *describabilia'* (i.e., described). So, just as *landscapes* are the structural possibilities actual 3-D countrysides present to painters who aspire to set out what is 'true to life' (in painted landscapes!), *facts* are those structural possibilities within (infinitely) diverse varieties of subject matters such that scientists who aspire to do so may succeed in stating of those subject matters what is 'true of life' (in their systems of statements of fact!).

So, 'taking cognizance of the facts' is much more than simulating and emulating a hypersensitive data receptor. On the other hand, it also seems to be more than just the clamping of a scientific theory's rules and definitions upon the world, thereby selecting of study only those subject matters which are 'cooperative' with the extant theories. Rather, 'the facts' emerge here as the world's possibilities for *being* described in some available language—which possibilities will be every bit as 'theory-laden' as the descriptions themselves are disclosed to be. (Could '$E = mc^2$' have expressed a fact a million years ago? For whom?) And this will be so whether those descriptions concern only simple color-registrations, as in titrations, or intricate subtle number-assignments, as within most standard cases of measurement.

Measurement

Once again the inclination is to view science's subject matters as chunks of the world, as 'out there'—
reposed, quiescent, and richly bedecked with properties—passively awaiting our theodolites, telescopes,
microscopes, balances, centrifuges, galvanometers,
accelerators, etc. As the camera records what is
posed and exposed in front of the lens to *be* recorded,
so (apparently) these instruments of measurement
objectively register and record the degrees to which
certain objects, processes, and events possess and
manifest certain properties.

Without doubt, what is derisively designated as
'dust-bowl empiricism' derives some of its appeal
from such an uncriticized view of the nature of
measurement. Only during the scientific revolutions
of this century—Relativity Theory and in Quantum
Mechanics—have modifications of such a pervasive,
powerful, and perennial view been lastingly effected.
When practical operationalists (like Mach and Einstein and Bridgman) began searching for the 'cash
value' of terms like *mass* and simultaneity and *time,*
a certain 'involvement' of subject matter and observer became clear. 'Interaction' is now the watch-
word.

What is it to say, as all celestial mechanicians before 1900 would have felt it meaningful to say, that
an explosion in Alpha Centuari took place 'at the
same time' as did some event here on earth (e.g.,

the eruption of Vesuvius)? True or false, such a claim would have at least seemed significant to everyone at Maxwell's Cavendish Laboratory. Since a photon of light emitted from Alpha Centauri would take over four of our years to traverse the distance to us, the synchronization of timepieces, and the calibration of all associated optical instrumentation, would present a calculational-computational problem of the greatest magnitude. The techniques of measurement used in so (relatively) simple a case traverse acres of physical theory, much of which would be 'built into' the 'measurement' which resulted. Just as Archimedes' principle can never be refuted by measurements made with a beam balance, nor Hooke's law falsified *via* readings rendered by a spring balance—these laws being the *basis* of these balances—so also nothing involving *terrestrial* chronometry and optical theory is going to be upset during our measurements of explosive disturbances near Alpha Centauri. These traditional disciplines are 'enshrined' within our measurements of celestial events. Whatever information our instruments *do* convey to us is what it is because such disciplines are the vehicle for interpretation of needle-deflections, signal-strengths and counter-clicks. To that extent there is a pervasive interaction between such events and our theories of measuring technique. Whatever numbers emerge from measuring encounters may be the result not of simple, objective data-registration, but of a most intricate enravelment of subject matter, probe, and theory.

(Somewhat like using porpoises to gather information about whales! or like using treacle droplet-probes to gather information about hot syrup!)

Little need be added here to the immense literature concerning the quantum theory of measurement. Only note this again: that information from the microphysical world reaches us in units no smaller than h (the quantum of action), and is always and necessarily the result of an interaction between some microphenomenon and a macroexperimental probe. Since the effect of the probe on the phenomenon is incalculable (in principle), our information must always be related to the *system* of phenomenon-*plus*-detector—information which, again, is restricted to event units greater than h.

It does not follow from this, of course, that knowledge which accrues to us from such measurements is no longer 'objective'. Rather, we must now recognize that 'objectivity' (in its classical meaning) may no longer be an appropriate conception for isolated (i.e., detector-independent) particles and processes. It is always a system, an ensemble, of processes about which we gain objective knowledge in microscience today. Perhaps the idea that once we were able to obtain more than just ensemble-knowledge (i.e., knowledge of microindividuals), was itself unsound? We have displaced the notion of measurement, nudged it from its unexamined pinnacle of classical objectivity, to a turbulent flux of detector-and-detected—and even to an occasional deep of inconstant subjectivity.

Again, the reasonable way courses midway between: objectivity is no less available to us today than it was to our predecessors. But it can no longer be construed as an objectivity of isolated particulars 'out there', a construction that was always unjustified. Just as sociologists *can* report objectively about groups of which they are members, so also laboratory detectors can report objectively about intricate situations within which they are inextricably entwined and intertwined. Nothing in our responsible conceptions of what inductive science is will require radical modification because of this 'realistic' appraisal of measurement. Scientific measuring instruments are not passive blotters; but neither are they so disturbing that they churn subject matters like eggbeaters. Rather, they record the properties of complex phenomena by disturbing them in a controlled and largely calculable way. The surgeon must cut to cure; the experimental scientist must dislodge and perturb in order to learn of a subject matter's properties when unperturbed and 'according to nature'.

Induction

I once remarked of a senior scientist that he had had forty years of experience. A critic rejoined that the individual in question did *not* have forty years' experience; rather, he had had the *same* experience over and over, forty years in a row. Is induction simply a rote repetition of stimulus and response, of anterior events followed by later events? Or can one *learn* something from induction—learn something about the *nature* of, and interconnections between, the phenomena before us, and not simply how they are sequentially distributed? Is induction a superficial survey of event-pairs, or does it permit us to peer 'inside' processes—to see what *makes* them 'tick', and not merely that they *do* 'tick'!

If *this* x is y, and *that* x is y, and those, and those, and those—indeed, if *all* x's ever encountered have also been y, will the claim '*all x are y*' be just a kind of actuarial shorthand for saying quickly what experience has revealed at length, *seriatim* and in detail? Or will '*all x are y*' reveal something 'deeper' than we could have learned just through repetitive experience—something to the effect that there is something '*y*-ish' about each x? Every possible position on this spectrum has been entertained by philosophers partisan to one polar extreme or to the other. Reichenbach congratulates Hume for having been the first to recognize that all induction, however intricate and 'theoretical', is ultimately dependent upon 'inductio per enumerationem simplicem' (Reichenbach, *Experience and Prediction*, p. 389). On the other hand, Aristotle, and a millennium of Aristotelians, urge that from noting *this* x to be a *y*, and *that* one, and *those* too—one can become conceptually positioned to make 'an inductive leap' to the (unrestricted) conclusion '*all x are y*', which latter somehow discloses the *essence* of x. For Aristotle, induction reveals that 'it is in the nature' of an x to be y; this cannot be a matter of logical necessity, of course, but it is, nonetheless, an unexceptional feature of the constitution of the actual world in which we live (Aristotle, *Posterior Analytics,* Book II, ch. 19).

On this issue, as on most others, philosophies of science divide into (1) 'philosophies of nothing but', (2) 'philosophies of something more', and (3) 'philosophies of what's what'. Inductive generalizations (even when stated as Laws of Nature), are *nothing but* empirical expressions which sum over enormous ranges of repeated observation-pairs (1). Or, induction may be represented as a process through which, by experience, we learn something of the fundamental structure of objects, events, and processes— where this 'fundamental something' is always qualitatively more than is disclosed *via* mere repetition (2). [Human beings *learn* about nature through induction—they come to understand it; animals and machines do not (although they may gather a great deal concerning how best to avoid mishaps and how to function efficiently.)]

The reasonable way (3) again seems to lie between mere instance-enumeration, on the one hand, and mysterious essence-divining, on the other. Perhaps just by noting that induction is rarely undertaken aimlessly, without some theoretically determined objective, it will become clear that generalizations are usually built on experience which is itself already highly selective. Scientists are not like manufacturers of ball-bearing toy skates. It is not 'quality and quantity control' but *understanding* which is (or should be) science's primary objective. This was long reflected in the reference to physics

as 'natural philosophy'—a scientific discipline which
has always required learning what is the case concerning classes of phenomena earmarked, by experience and by theory, for further reflection and
study. We learn what obtains within phenomena—
what 'makes them go'—by way of our perceptual
linkages with the world through sense experience.
We *understand* those experiences, even when they
occur in profuse and diverse arrays, only when we
can pattern them within conceptual frameworks;
these provide structures to 'the scientific mind', idea-
structures which are *sometimes* related to the structures of processes 'out there' in the actual subject
matter. Induction is thus an epistemic tube; if phenomena come through it in pairs, or in trios, etc.,
often enough, then they may be recognized as not
'merely accidental' vis-à-vis their correlation. But
the tube still has to be *aimed* in a given direction of
inquiry, just as a telescope must be intentionally
'pointed' (for some purpose) at some restricted por-
tion of the sky. It is such nonaccidental features of
our inquiries into the world which, when understood,
render whole classes of phenomena intelligible. Such
guided uses of induction, however, have made modern scientific experimentation a virtual embodiment
of theoretical understanding—for every datum encountered is detected along a line of inquiry, within
a framework of interest bounded by the criteria of
relevance and significance which aims our efforts
this way rather than *that* way. Experiments may indeed be 'the senses extended'. But sharp eyes without a quick brain make Jack a dull idiot—a 'telescope

flailer'. Ingenious experimentation, without the constant control of careful theory, could soon overstock laboratories with 'number-finders', but leave them somewhat short on new directions for the scientific understanding. "The discovery of new facts is open to any blockhead with patience, and manual dexterity and acute senses" (Sir William Hamilton).

Experiment

For Galileo experimentation was important, but only as an *ex post facto* display and confirmation of what (for him) had already been disclosed by reason. Once the world, as created by God-the-Mathematician, had surrendered itself up for geometrical description, its miniscule properties and hidden details were epistemically foreordained—just as are all the consequences within Euclidean geometry for any student who accepts the Axioms and the Rules. Then, setting out a lively demonstration of those truths (with sloping boards, pulleys, and wires) was about as necessary in natural philosophy as it was within geometry—namely, not at all. Such recourse was mainly for those too slow-witted to follow the argument. Still, Galileo would have viewed it as a cardinal sin for anyone who was unable to follow the argument *also* to have ignored the 3-D 'experiment'. Some of his contemporaries did just that—and, in so doing, they sinned against reason. For although the structure of experience was construed as geometrically designed, that same design was clearly *in* the experiment, just as it was also in the *argu-*

ment which articulated the structure of that experiment. (This echoes our earlier remarks on the concept of *scene*.) Physical reality appeared as a geometrical creation for Galileo; physical facts were structured *à la* Euclid. Phenomena, experimentation, and argumentation could all share the same structure. Indeed, they *must* do so even to be related as subject matter—demonstration—and description. So the same insights seemed available to the natural philosopher by either one of two different routes of inquiry: geometrical argumentation or laboratory experimentation. The structure of physical facts could be delineated by either kind of inquiry. Even so, for Galileo (as for many contemporary scientific heroes) the 'rightness' of an experiment, of its design, was to some extent disclosed in the degree to which it embodied purely theoretical arguments. The failure of experimental results to support anterior theoretical reflections—this has always been, for some, an initial indication of something wrong in the experimental design itself. Herein lies the power of *gedankenexperiments,* such as Galileo's Pisa-cannon-balls, Newton's bucket, Einstein's elevator, Schrödinger's cat, etc.; the theoretical issues in such examples just overwhelm the virtues of pushing or pulling or cutting or heating chunks of matter in order to *show* 'what is the case' to the unconvinced.

Contrast this view of experiment with a diametrically different one. The position parodied as 'dust-bowl empiricism' construes experimentation and controlled observation as the very source, the development and the fulfillment, of everything worthwhile in science. All else is "mere speculation", or even "metaphysics"! In extreme form a scientist so oriented will 'let the facts speak for themselves'; he will tinker, roam, and ruminate at random, giving 'the world' (i.e., his chosen subject matter) every opportunity to 'express itself'. Scientific theories, on this account, will be like X-ray photographs of what given subject matters reveal of themselves during careful, precise, quantitatively circumscribed experimental inquiry. Experimentation provides its own direction, on this view. Preconceptions, hypotheses, hunches, intuitions, and errant speculations will, apparently, be pulped beneath the relentless advance of such an experimenter. Instrumental accuracy, control, mensurational detail—these will become the criteria and the very consummation of careful inquiry, alongside which all the elaborate, clever constructions of abstract theoreticians fade into the oblivion of history (and even mythology).

How is it possible to articulate either of the above positions without a modicum of caricature? Caricature or not, there *is* a contrast to be drawn between such extreme conceptions of the nature and function of controlled laboratory experience. The one view is that excellence in experimentation lies at the terminus of successful theorizing—as a final corroboration of what reason suggests to be the case. On this account the experimenter is directed by considerations of how the processes he is contriving to set into motion are relevant to some conceptual framework, the latter being central to whether or not we *understand* a given subject matter. Experiment here is theory-laden, theory-directed, and theory-oriented. It is simply the probe which ideas, concept-clusters, and arguments extend into actual, 3-D subject matters. On the other account, however, theory is the *product* of experimentation. It is just the terse, elegant, symbolic embodiment of what the theoretician has extracted from out of the writhing, multi-parametric subject matter itself. Here the theorist is subject to the judgments of the experimenter. The latter will always be 'letting the facts speak for themselves', and will be rendering them as perspicuous as possible. The theoretician, in straining to 'see the reality beneath the facts', might sometimes suppress what is all too obvious in the experiment—searching beyond for the 'something more'. But such a quest too often exceeds what experience can sanction. Thus this is a counsel of restraint against unbridled theorizing. The creative imagination must always 'knuckle under' to the data, the evidence, the facts. One way of ensuring this may be to stress the 'shorthand' function of theories; i.e., they are just systematically neat description-sets.

Again, history of science supports both positions. Hoyle's steady state theory has just given ground before a fusillade of facts from quasar astronomy. Eddington's second edition of *Fundamental Theory* records the 'fine structure constant' as related to the number *137*—in accord with certain observations made after the first edition was published. Without warning he thereby modified the first edition, where the constant was theoretically determined to be related to the number *136!* Mesons turned out *not* to be 'electrons with queer properties at high energies', as some theorists had urged (Wilson and Blackett, 1936). Electromagnetic radiation turned out *not* to be uniformly continuous and undulatory—extant theory to the contrary notwithstanding (Planck, 1901). On the other hand, there was in fact a trans-Uranic planet (Neptune), just as theory required (Leverrier and Adams, 1846). There have been multiform discovered things like neutrinos (Pauli, 1929), positrons (Dirac, 1931), antiprotons, and antineutrons (Segre *et al.*, 1956), as well as the planet Pluto (Tombaugh, 1931)—all as theory required. Finding very often requires knowing where to look, the former being a function of the latter—experimental discovery being a function of theoretical strategy.

So it would appear that the verdict of history of science is impartial as between these two philosophical claimants. Examples of (1) theory leading experiment by the nose, and of (2) experiment correcting, and even generating, theory—such are ample enough within the ancestry of science. The *via media* is thus somewhat difficult to discern in this context. But clearly there can be no 'all or nothing' and *final* philosophical answer to the question 'What is experiment?' *Experimentation as demonstration of, or as corroboration of, theory* is surely different from *experiment as a generative source of theory.* When laboratory activities are this diverse, it is idle to seek a single philosophical formula to embrace everything called 'experiment'. Better to explore each case of inquiry on its own merits, learning thereby what epistemological or semantical or methodological role *this* individual experiment may have played relative to *this* particular theory. (A single given experiment may impinge upon different theories in quite distinct ways; it may bear on the same theory in different ways at different times.) Better also to ask how *this* theory may have been supported, defined and clarified by that particular experiment. (A given theory may relate to a host of independent experiments in a host of conceptually different ways.) What a monumental mistake it is, therefore, to seek some quasi-causal connection operative always between the design of an experiment and the creation of a theory. As if the idea of *cause* were sufficiently clear even at the level of billiard balls! It is not. *Eo ipso* it is not generally clear how experiments cause theories to possess certain properties, nor how theories cause experiments to have whatever design characteristics they may manifest.

Causality

A funny thing happened to 'cause' on its way from the Lyceum. Aristotle's word, αἰτία, as we still find traces of it in terms like 'aetiology', was beautifully articulated in The Philosopher's Doctrine of the Four Causes. Therein Aristotle was concerned with the reasons for, or the explanations of, distinguishable aspects of particular happenings. Of the massive Mayan earthwork structure which houses Yale's Tandem Van der Graff Accelerator one could be ex-

pected to ask 'why?' (Frank Lloyd Wright's constant question.)

Why what?

What *is* the question? Is one concerned to know
what that great mound *is?* What is it meant to
achieve? (John Dewey's constant question.) What
is inside of it; how is it designed? What makes it all
'go'? (James Clerk Maxwell's constant question.)
Of what material is it constituted? These are re-
quests for an explanation of the genesis, the design,
the *modus operandi* and the objectives of this im-
posing scientific addition to the Ivy. And the cloven
hooves of (1) *material,* (2) *efficient,* (3) *formal,* and
(4) *final* causation are clearly chiselled into such
questioning.

1. "Explain to me what the 'Emperor' accelerator
   is made of—the metals, crystals, plastics, etc." Is
   there any wood in its construction? Or silk? Or
   animal fibers?
2. "What is the reason for the heavy earthen mound
   over the great instrument?" Why not a thinner,
   more appealing-to-the-eye metallic shell? Why
   not reinforced concrete?
3. "Make me understand how such an accelerator
   works, its design." Is it like a synchro-cyclotron?
   How does it differ from Stanford's linear accelerator?
4. "What are the expectations, the intended accom-
   plishments, of such a machine? What did Yale and
   the NSF hope to achieve?" What will we have

learned by 1975 which, without Emperor, we should not have suspected?

Aristotle's *Metaphysics* journeyed to the Near East, from whence it was slowly percolated northwest to Latin-thinking lands—considerably the worse for its orientation. αἰτία became rendered as *causa,* a term which in ancient Latin has much the same significance of the original Greek term; that is, the four *causae* also concern explanations of, or reasons for, things being as we find them to be—their aetiology. The Scientific Revolution, however, had a forceful effect upon our general understanding of the nature of causation. Efficient causation—the 'go' of things, the pushes and pulls, the drives and linkages, the perturbations and deflections—snared the attention of most philosophers, and became so energetically articulated within the emerging sciences of Descartes, Galileo, Barrow, Newton, and Leibniz that it by now seems extraordinarily difficult to think of causation in any sense other than that focused upon in the expression 'efficient causation'. Philosophers still become perplexed concerning what kind of *efficient* causation, final causation really is! What kind of 'nudges from astern' are material and formal causation? Due to such anxious confusions final causation (a pull from the future?), was banished peremptorily from natural science; material and formal causations were discussed, if at all, only *sotto voce*. Indeed, the whole *idea* of causation developed in remarkably Baconian terms, in the sense that x was construed as the cause of y if and only if

the existence of x could 'bring about' the existence
of y, or if the absence of x could prevent the presence
of y. A cause came to be thought of as a trigger; you
caused y when you contrived to bring about a chain
of events which terminated in y. There is no dearth
of this 'Rube Goldberg' notion of causal chain effi-
cacy even in the recent history of experimental science. (See N. R. Hanson, "Causal Chains," in *Mind*,
1955.) The challenge too often is that of seeking to
fabricate in the laboratory complex conditions which
seemed before to obtain only in nature. Wohler's
laboratory synthesis of urea was a triumph of experimental science because, through its ingenious
precision, its controlled and quantitative care, a sub-
stance was produced which had theretofore been
construed as beyond human contrivance. Similarly
with some large proteins, and a few short-lived mi-
croparticles. Ultimately, experimental science has
come to seem to some an enormous 'Erector Set'
challenge such that, by analysis and decomposition
of natural events, men can conspire to construct corresponding events in the laboratory—finally to
'bring about' whatever 'natural' state of affairs one
could adequately describe. Or, in experimental medi-
cine, the challenge often appears to be to analyze a
malady such that the appropriate *breaking* of a link
in the 'causal chain' will prevent some bodily mal-
function. Either way, the conceptual intimacy between all scientific experiment and 'causal chain'
laboratory productions has suggested to some
thinkers that science be construed as a sophisticated
engineering operation, replete with levers, triggers,

wires, pulleys, circuits—indeed all the paraphernalia that science in the Michelson-Millikan tradition does actually require! The creative scientific imagination may just be our scientists'. ability to imagine laboratory conditions which will create naturally appearing phenomena (e.g., urea, lightning, chemo-luminescence).

Yet, there must be 'something more' to this kind of account. The request for the cause of an event is still a request for some *explanation* of that event. It is a plea for understanding—a plea that the event in question be rendered comprehensible in terms of other 'unsurprisabilia' known to obtain. (As Peirce intimates, a perplexity X is explained when it is shown to follow "as a matter of course" from the unperplexing y and z.) The 'dust-bowl' conception of causality blows away before a simple example like this: An airplane crashes; the pilot is killed; the FAA seeks for the *cause* of the accident.

Consider the possibilities:

1. The engine stopped, at night, over the Rockies.
2. Insufficient care had been given, during the last 100-hour inspection, to the fuel strainers, which *post mortem* examination proved to be clogged.
3. The pilot had probably not acquainted himself with meteorological conditions en route; at least the FAA Flight Service has no record of his having done so.
4. The weather data broadcast during the fatal flight was not current for the locale of the disaster.

5. Local thunderstorms hampered radio reception and transmission.

6. The pilot was not in practice vis-à-vis night flying and instrument procedures; his log book records his most recent night flight as having taken place 6 months previously.

7. Financial and personal anxieties affected the overall state of the aviator's psyche: so testifies his next of kin.

Now *all* these states of affairs could obtain simultaneously. Within suitable and specific frames of inquiry each one of references (1)–(7) cited above could be designated as *the cause* of the accident. To the aircraft designer stoppage of the engine was the cause. (It won't fly without power.) To the repair station supervisor shortcomings in the inspection procedure led to the accident. (The engine won't run without fuel.) To the psychologist pilot-anxieties were at fault. (A man can't 'think instruments' with a brain soaked in worry.) To the FAA flight examiner the lack of recent practice was responsible. (Rusty pilots, like rusty nails, don't drive well.) What counts as *the cause* of such an event will, in most cases, be that happening which (within a given framework of orientation—aeronautical, familial, legal, psychological) will render it intelligible that the accident took place at all. Such specialist-examiners as these will designate some anterior state (i.e., the clogged strainer, the lack of proficiency, the anxiety, etc.), concluding therefrom that the ensuing accident was 'all but inevitable', given such an antecedent preparation as that.

Thus the assignment of a cause is also a highly 'theory-laden' undertaking. Extensive networks of theoretical concern overlap upon the event in question. It is then a matter of the specialist's own theoretical posture, his interests, and his immediate professional concern which will load the very language used in his description of the accident with 'proto-explanations', with tacit semantical commitments, any one of which may make the event intelligible for someone—the natural terminus of some sequence of happenings.

Once granting all this, however, the pushing and pulling, the linkages and feedbacks—all so dear to the 'causal chain' view of experimentation—these fade before a more sophisticated conception of science, one which seems to concern only earlier and later states of affairs, theoretically construed.

> Charge separation? Discharge!
> Satellite deceleration? Fall to earth!
> Tilt airfoil up? Increase drag! Etc.

This has become so apparent within theoretical physics that the very notion of *cause* has virtually been exorcised. Consider astrophysics and cosmology, within which disciplines the mathematical treatment of 'cause' and 'effect' is indistinguishable from calculations involving the time parameter t; state descriptions of events at $t - \Delta t$, and $t + \Delta t$ are construed as doing everything for science that 'traditional talk' of causes and effects used to do. Since a designating of the *causes* of a phenomenon is itself a theory-vectored performance, any careful explication of the full theory, plus detailed references to earlier and later states of the phenomenon in question, *must* be operationally equivalent to our more anthropomorphic ordinary language—that involving physical exertion in pursuit of physical goals. Much of our causal discourse derives from the recognition that events are often *effective.* (*Human beings* are effective, sometimes, in bringing about what they desire. But are other agencies within the cosmos similarly effective, for similar reasons? Do extragalactic processes cause specific things to happen as *desired?* As *they* desire?)

Within quantum mechanics the 'de-contentization' of causal talk has gone even further. It is not just that somewhat less anthropomorphic chat has been substituted for 'classical' causal discourse inside microphysics; rather, the very logic of microparticulate state descriptions is in many ways *incompatible* with the conceptual framework which structures our everyday ('classical') thinking about causes and effects. That is, *complete* state descriptions (i.e., 3 sharp spatial coordinates, plus a precise specification of energy) of individual particles at times t, $t - \Delta t$, and $t + \Delta t$—these are wholly ruled out of quantum mechanics by the 'formal rules' which structure that complex discipline. *Partial* state descriptions of microphenomena ('partial' as against the 'completeness' possible in a classical sense) constitute the maximal theoretical and epistemological possibilities within contemporary microphysics. As a matter of the *logic* of quantum mechanics, there is a theoretical limit to the joint precision obtainable for each of two conjugate parameters, such as *time* and *energy* (Heisenberg, 1927) or *position* (P) and *momentum* (M) (Bohr, von Neumann and Dirac, 1928). The latter parameters are treated as operators within a noncommutative algebra such that $PM - MP = n$ (some number other than 0) (Graves, 1854). It should be stressed, again, that this is not merely technological limitation—something resulting only from the gross crudity of our present probes. It is, rather, a feature of the rule-network—the formal concept-framework—of the mathematical algorithm of quantum mechanics. The complete state descriptions required in classical cause-and-effect relationships demand a thoroughgoing commutativity between all dynamical operators, such that it is theoretically irrelevant whether one determines first a bullet's velocity and then its position, or vice versa. This independence of dynamical operators constitutes a possibility totally excluded from the formalism of any workable version of quantum mechanics set out during the past forty years, e.g., those of von Neumann and Dirac, 1930–1935. (Some 'systems' of microphysics have been speculated about, systems which abrogate these 'Uncertainty Relations'; but they turn out to be so badly attuned to the experimental facts that they should not be called 'quantum mechanics' at all. The author sees no reason for not including in this category the work of De Broglie, Bohm, Vigier, Bopp, Janossy, and Alexandrov. The parallel philosophical speculations

of Popper, Feyerabend, Mehlberg, Toulmin, and
other 'counter-Copenhagen' interpreters might also
be noted here as being somewhat out of touch with
the experimental realities of contemporary Elemen-
tary Particle physics.)

What is the philosophical upshot of such an oscil-
lation between the chainlike conception of causality
("For want of a nail the shoe was lost; for want of
a shoe the horse was lost ... all for want of a nail.")
as against an abstract representation of theoretical
parameters such as typifies modern physics, within
a classical concept of causality, is difficult even to de-
tect? It is just this: what is even to *count* as a causal
connection between phenomena within any context
always depends upon one's special queries concerning the subject matter in question. That is, a single
event-sequence 'viewed' via two different theories,
might suggest quite different candidates for the
status of the *cause* and the *effect*. (The "cause" of
conflict in Vietnam has been assigned to notoriously
many and diverse situations and individuals.) Moreover, some theories seem not to require the causal
ideas at all!

Perhaps the 'middle way' here would be just to
acknowledge that much of our everyday experience,
our thinking, and our discourse, *does* depend upon
classical conceptions of causality. (Magistrates,
policemen, mechanics and plumbers cannot afford
the luxuries of algebraic abstraction.) Laboratory
experience 'links up' at many points with such everyday experience; to that extent it will always seem (to
some degree) natural for scientists to discern and

identify those linkages between experiences inside and outside the laboratory (where the causality concept is most applicable). Thus even in those theories in which *cause* and *effect* are very much modified concepts, or even dispensed with altogether, when such theories make contact with laboratory experimentation and observation (as ultimately they *must* do), there will be a human tendency to accommodate theoretical discourse to classical notions of causality—even when doing so can be somewhat misleading. The universal design *may* be that of a pulsing, organismic abstraction; but our representations of it, like our talk about it, will always 'click-click' off in single-file orderings of words, formulas, descriptions, and experiments. This is part of the price science pays for analysis. For analysis of complex wholes must be unit by unit. *We* are beings who are effective to the degree that we can cause things to come about, piece by piece, as we please. This is true also in scientific laboratories and for much the same reason. When our theories, however abstract, are linked with activities in the laboratory (as they must be, sooner or later, in order to be intelligible to us sentients), further associations with the causal nexus are inevitable.

But what is semantically inevitable in the course of explaining natural phenomena need not be pernicious, not so long as we remain aware that our explications of microtheories and macrotheories via causal talk could be misleading if construed as being literally true of the theory's conceptual fine-structure. Causal discourse seems to be most effective

when explaining phenomena 'across' languages—
when discussing quantum mechanics with engineers,
or general relativity with amateur astronomers. It is
sometimes dubious as an explanatory reference
within a single language. Dirac and Heisenberg have
no need of the causal hypothesis when discussing
with each other the present state of their perplexing
art.

Explanation

Causal explanations are important to us. There are,
of course, many other ways of rendering phenomena
understandable. A drawing of the heart is not a
causal explanation. But philosophical controversy
concerning explanation has often placed causal explanation at the forefront.

What is it to explain a perplexing natural phenomenon? Within a diversity of answers to this question, the thesis of Hempel and Oppenheim deserves
special attention.

Many well-educated persons are still capable of
being surprised when, after casual star-gazing for
a few nights, they note a bright point of light to have
come to a halt, and then to move in the direction
opposite to its original course. Even today such
individuals might request an explanation of so star-
tling an observation. What can they be told? A modicum of heliostatic planetary theory will be gestured
at, of course, with some inevitable Newtonian asides.
Then some further, specific, references will be made
concerning the joint-distribution of the planets, and

stars, as they appeared on the celestial globe at some earlier moment in time. This 'state description' of the planetary array at $t - \Delta t$, plus some understanding of the dynamics of our local system, will quite often resolve the perplexity and allay the surprise of our sky gazer. For what had seemed problematic was then inferentially linked to prior conditions, none of which was in any way problematic. The retrogradation follows "as a matter of course" (Peirce). Psychologically it then appears that explaining some surprising x consists in decomposing it into smaller elements each one of which reflects some previous commitment totally lacking in surprise or novelty of any kind. Philosophically this may be put, as Hempel put it, by noting that an anomaly is explained by tracing it back, through laws, to initial conditions established through observation. (This is a kind of logician's analogue to 'causal chain' thinking. Thus, if the *cause* of the kingdom's collapse can be traced back to the want of a nail in a horseshoe, then the explanation of the kingdom's collapse consists in tracing back through a statement-series until one reaches a premise from which the entire series is generable—including the consequence that the kingdom will collapse.)

But if *that* is what explaining consists in, then one might have *predicted* the 'anomaly' earlier when, while confronted with initial conditions and Laws, it could have been deduced that, e.g., the planet would appear to halt and then move 'backwards'—just as we can now predict that a Piper Cub will appear to move backwards from the window of a Boeing-707!

Since what is predictable can hardly be anomalous, explaining x becomes tantamount to showing that x is predictable, i.e., could have been predicted! Premisses describing observations at $t - \Delta t$ entail conclusions describing events at $t + \Delta t$.

Explanation and *prediction* are thus conceptually linked within the Hempel-Oppenheim account. Explaining x is predicting x after it has actually happened. (Clearly, the predictable is not a matter for perplexity.) Predicting x is explaining it before it has actually happened. (What could be more predictable than a recurrent phenomenon which is non-problematic?) Moreover, this relationship between the concepts of *prediction* and *explanation* must be 'managed' within a deductive framework—a theory. The latter allows one to infer from initial conditions (through laws) to predictions of future states. It also permits one to reason from observed anomalies, 'back' through laws, to initial conditions whose lack of novelty leaves nothing to be perplexed about, at least not within the original context of inquiry. (The 'arrow of inference' has a different 'sense' within these two undertakings. Inferring to conclusions from known premisses is radically different from 'inferring to', or 'reasoning towards' premisses from known conclusions. Of this more later.)

This analysis reduces questions about explanation and prediction to questions concerning whether or not there are *deductive connections* between anomalies and initial conditions—whether, that is, there exists a theory within whose systematic capillaries one's surprise can be deployed, diverted, scattered, and diluted. Big question marks disappear when one attends to the sharp inkdots of which they are constituted.

Several critics have argued that this makes of theories little more than inferential connecting-rods, or connecting-reticula. *Any* calculus which allows one to 'predict' future states of affairs (however strange the theory and incomprehensible the future state) would thereby also be the instrument through which explanations of those future states must also proceed. The way is open, apparently, for all manner of 'nutty' correlation-schemes such that whatever (e.g., increased sunspot activity) inclines us to predict some future state (e.g., a wheat failure in Kansas) would thereby also have provided the conduitry for explaining the latter. Dissatisfaction with this has been expressed by many philosophers; Schoolmen anxious over the fallacy of 'post hoc ergo propter hoc' would have been predictably anxious over Hempel's account. Many philosophers are not content to construe theories merely as 'predicting calculi'. Still less will they grant that an anomaly has been explained when one merely designates other conditions from the obtaining of which that event could have been predicted (e.g., from the distant storm warning we may predict the high winds; but are the high winds 'explained' by the storm warning? Are they explained by the cumulus mammatus and nimboid clouds everywhere above?)

Since we have found some point in contrasting radically empirical attitudes toward a scientific conception (e.g., observation) with alternative abstract treatments, it might be worth attempting that again. The Hempel-Oppenheim account of *explanation* and *prediction* is surely a theoretician's delight. It suggests that an explaining of x is not a rubbing of one's nose into x, or an attempt to empathize with the 'pure essence' of x. Rather it is an inferential-linking of x with a variety of other non-problematic data, or data-claims. This delineates an important feature of theories themselves; linking the unfamiliar with the familiar has always been a glory of theoretical science.

Now, what empirical counterposture is to be adopted in contrast to the relatively formalistic and abstract analysis of Hempel? Perhaps it is this: there is no substitute for old-fashioned familiarity when one seeks to understand a subject matter. Truly, there is little to be explained (at least about fish) to the old fisherman who, like his father and grandfather before him, has lived all his life with net and hook, gaff and oar. What questions will perplex *him?* What will the twenty-year-old ichthyologist explain to *him?* There is something the old sea captain has which the young fluid mechanician lacks. There is something the experienced electrical repairman surely has which the junior electrodynamicist may lack. Deep and abiding familiarity with a subject matter can render it totally understood, unproblematic and comprehensible—sometimes in the face of a total lack of theoretical or inferential sophistication. Midwives do not have records remarkably inferior to that of M.D.s. Or will we say that the ancient mariner, since he lacks calculational skill in hydrodynamics, therefore does not understand the sea around him, and could not explain its properties to others? That would be too absurd. Must we pronounce the midwife too ignorant of the process of childbirth fully to comprehend the vital drama being enacted before her eyes? Doesn't the senior electrician even know what he is doing? Is the algebra of electron theory *that* critical to his work?

Thus the suspicion of some philosophers that explanation (in Hempel's sense) may be possible without understanding. They find the equation 'Premiss for X = Explanation of X' repugnant. And in our counterpoised empirical view, understanding may be possible in the absence of any 'Hempelian' explanation. Anatomists are not notorious as keen arguers. Perhaps this latter point need not be taken too seriously, however; a pancreatic sympathy should never be confused with articulate and detailed understanding. Nijinsky understood the dance. But, apparently, he could not explain it to others. He was inarticulate about it; others could not understand *from what he said* what the dance was! Similarly the Wright brothers understood flight; but they were largely inarticulate with respect to it. Others could hardly gather, from their words, what flight was. The brothers were powerless to make them see. Our midwife, electrician, and fisherman *could not explain* (to others) childbirth, circuitry, and seasonal spawning. The *sentiment of comprehension* should therefore never be confused with the *structure of explanation*. *Feeling* and *logic* are as different as *brain* and *mind*. *Knowing how* and *knowing that* are as unlike as *retinal reaction* and *observing*. The distinction between understanding in the sense of intuitive familiarity and understanding in the sense of rationally comprehending the 'go' of things must never be collapsed.

Still, the middle way might again be the one which seeks to gain strength from both positions. What can be wrong with our seeking examples of scientific theory which are capable both of explaining *à la* Hempel and of providing understanding and illumination of the nature of the phenomena in question? Even if distinguishable, the two are genuinely worthwhile objectives for scientific enquiry; they are wholly compatible. And, it may be noted, the second is unattainable without the first. So although Hempel's account of scientific explanation may not be sufficient, it seems to be necessary. Ontological insight, unstructured by quantitatively precise argument and analysis, is mere speculation at best, and navel-contemplatory twaddle at worst.

Theories

In his *Syntaxis Mathematica,* Claudius Ptolemy put together a detailed calculational scheme of prediction. It was quantitatively accurate to a degree unsurpassed until late in the sixteenth century. Predictions of the future positions of the planets were thus genuine inferential possibilities within Ptolemy's astronomy. But, by his own account, and by way of subsequent criticisms advanced by timid heliocentrists and Schoolmen, no explanation, no understanding, no comprehension of the planets, and their interrelationships, was forthcoming from the hand or mind of Ptolemy. His positional astronomy was restricted to studying the kinematics of otherwise inscrutable lights in the sky. Understanding that they moved, and that scholars were able roughly to predict where they would move to, was totally different from understanding *why* and *how* they moved as they did. Copernicus' heliocentric alternative was, at first, not as successful a predicting device as was Ptolemy's *Almagest*. But it did offer a theory, a conceptual framework, an idea-structure within which one seemed able to relate the actual behavior and appearances of the planets (i.e., their observed kinematics) with a physical account of what sort of things such objects really were. What has percolated through to us is the Copernican recognition that our understanding of what planets *are* is intimately connected with our ability to predict where they will be at future times, and to describe precisely where they are now.

So, in this historical example, we have an instance of two different theories (Ptolemy's and Copernicus') which were *not* equal in explanatory power, despite the fact that they were (for a short time) equally efficient as predicting machines. Put in another way: the inferential connections proposed by Ptolemy, despite their success in prediction, did not foster an understanding of the heavens to the same degree, nor in the same way, as did those inferential connections offered by Copernicus. Yet these latter were no more 'successful' in predictions than those within the Ptolemaic alternative (at least this obtained during the late sixteenth century).

At work here are different notions of the nature of scientific theories. What are theories? What are they supposed to do?

Hempel's account of explanation may be but a specialized reflection of an overall view of theories. If the major responsibility of a scientist is to supply statement-systems for deducing future state descriptions from earlier ones, then to speak of x as 'explained' is to say only that it has been located within an acceptable inference network. From *any* description over which the theory and its sundry laws range one should be able to infer to any other intratheoretic description whatsoever. (The inference may be *deductive*—toward the bottom of the page; or retroductive—toward the top.) But although this may be a necessary feature of any system of propositions 'properly' to be called "a theory", it is surely not a sufficient condition. It must always be logically possible for two theories, I and II, to be equally powerful in prediction yet wholly dissimilar vis-à-vis the degree to which they are felt to give an 'understanding' of their single subject matter. The astronomies of Ptolemy, Copernicus, and Brahe, as widely understood in A.D. 1600, were indistinguishable from the point of view of their forecasting capabilities. But that they constituted different idea-frameworks about the planets was clear enough within the intellectual revolutions of the seventeenth century. [Again, wave mechanics and matrix mechanics were shown to be predictively equivalent in 1926 (by

Eckardt and Schrödinger), and equivalent in an even stronger sense in 1930 (by Dirac, within his operator calculus). But Dirac himself has recently been lecturing to the effect that 'the conceptual pictures' provided by wave mechanics and matrix mechanics are so different as to make one of them far preferable to the other. The *understanding* of microphenomena provided by one is different from that afforded by the other—despite their indistinguishability at the level of observational number-production.]

In practice, therefore, distinctions *are* made between (1) theories that interlink descriptions within arbitrary inferential networks, and (2) different theories, the inferential linkages within which are patterned in terms of idea-clusters, analogies, and models such that to have succeeded *both* in inferring 'anomalies' from initial conditions (via the standard principles of deductive inference) and *also* to have placed that 'anomaly' within an intelligible framework of ideas (wherein further principles are now construed as 'laws of nature'), is to have *explained* the phenomenon in question in the fullest sense modern science can provide.

'How to succeed in prediction without ever explaining anything' is thus something more than a parody of the Hempel position. Rather, it indicates that view as not having said enough about explanation (and about scientific theory) to exclude *'mere* predicting devices' as being serious candidates for such titles. There *are* (and have always been) non-explaining predicting devices in the history of science; philosophers will insist on being shown how, on the Hempel theory—all of whose criteria are met, e.g., by Ptolemaic astronomy and by mere correlation studies in several disciplines—such nonexplaining predictors are yet to be excluded from the circle of genuine scientific explanations and scientific theories, in the fullest sense of those expressions. Hempel's view needs supplementation, not revision.

Laws

The framework that structures an explanatory scientific theory derives its shape from the Laws of Nature set high up in the deductively fertile realms of the algorithm. The understanding of a subject matter conveyed *via* a theory is connected with the idea-Gestalt packed into each law. Since laws such as $F = G^{(m_1\,m_2)}/r^2$ are replete with variable terms, they are not, like propositions, directly true or false. They are not propositions at all, but rather *propositional schema*. Of course, if the numerical values for each of the variables is specified, or if the entire expression is universally quantified, the result *will* be a proposition. It will then be true if it expresses a 'law of nature'. However, philosophers have learned that law-statements are not like ordinary statements in any significant way.

'Ordinary' empirical statements can be located in logical space by delineating their (1) Syntax, (2) Semantics, and (3) their Epistemological status.

Syntax (1) concerns what might be called 'sign-design'—such that to designate a proposition as 'synthetic' is to characterize the symbol-structure of that assertion. Thus S is *synthetic* if and only if its negation, not-S, entails no inconsistencies (i.e., nothing of the form Q *and* not-Q). Knowing this much about a proposition is, of course, not yet to know anything of its contingent truth or falsity; either S or not-S constitute logical possibilities: both are consistent. Reflection alone is thus insufficient to determine the truth value of S, or of not-S. Which brings us to the second, Semantical, point above.

Besides being synthetic, empirical claims are usually vulnerable; this is the locus of Semantics (2). There is nothing about any uninterpreted cluster of signs, whatever their structure, which relates to vulnerability or invulnerability in any sense. Sign-design *simpliciter* is sense-neutral. Some consideration of the *meaning* of symbols, such that on one interpretation a claim may be defeasible, while on another the possibility of counterevidence may be inconceivable—this is the thrust of the vulnerable-invulnerable dichotomy intended within (2) above. Invulnerable claims (whatever the genesis of that invulnerability) are often designated as 'necessary' or 'necessarily true.' Vulnerable claims, on the other hand, are said to be 'contingent', e.g., on the way the world is, or on the rules of the game, or on the conditions of inquiry within a given context.

Now, besides being constituted of a synthetic sign-design (1) and of a contingent (vulnerable) semantical status (2), empirical claims are such that the information they carry can be gained only through experience of one kind or another. Since reflection alone is insufficient to decide the truth or falsity of a synthetic/contingent claim, something else must be involved. *Experience* is that 'something else', which is clear from the attempts we make to justify such claims against all challenges to the contrary. Such a justification would be logically unlike that appropriate to demonstrating that, e.g., all equiangular triangles are equilateral.

Empirical propositions are, therefore, (1) synthetic, (2) contingent, and (3) *a posteriori*.

Other propositions, however, true or false in a genuine sense are different from empirical propositions in matters of syntax, semantics, and epistemological status. Claims like 'All fathers are parents', 'Bicycles have two wheels', and 'All equiangular triangles are equilateral' are (re: their sign-design) the opposite of synthetic. The denials of such claims generate inconsistencies—by which is meant no more, at this stage, than sign-designs of the form Q *and not-Q*. If such a sign-design as this is diametrically opposed to that set out earlier under the title 'synthetic', we might designate such a propositional state as 'analytic'. A proposition will then be analytic if and only if its negation *does* generate (via rules of the 'language' within which it figures) some symbol-cluster of the form Q *and not-Q*. (Nothing has been said yet about the semantical status (2) of S, or of Q *and not-Q*.)

Moreover, if synthetic claims are vulnerable, their opposites (i.e., 'analytic claims') might well be termed 'invulnerable'. This is the semantic force of 'necessary' or 'necessarily true' in most ordinary contexts. A claim such as 'all Euclidean equiangular triangles are equilateral', since nothing intelligible could count against it, will be felt to be necessarily true within the language (*L*) of which it is a part. Now this much goes beyond mere sign-design. For we are here noting that a necessary claim will, within *L,* always be *true. Truth* and *consistency* differ typically. So now it is not just the *form* of an assertion, but also the meaning of its terms (i.e., the semantical values inserted into the symbolic variables) which is at issue.

Tautologies (claims which cannot be false, and whose negations are inconsistent) are therefore (1) analytic, and (2) necessary—i.e., true by legislation.

Furthermore, such claims—if they *are* 'claims'— since reflection is sufficient to reveal their necessity, are what they are independently of experience. The 'knowledge' they convey is not drawn from experience. Their justification requires no appeal to experience. If 'a posteriori' indicated of empirical claims that they were epistemologically dependent upon experience, 'a priori' may indicate of tautologies that they are epistemologically independent of experience.

This much logic-chopping demarcates two kinds of propositions. On the one hand, we have empirical propositions that are synthetic, contingent, and *a posteriori.* On the other, we have tautologies that are analytic, necessary, and *a priori.* If laws of nature are expressed in proposition (and it would be hard to deny this; one feature of a law is that its linguistic articulation is invariably said to be of what is 'true'), then what *kind* of proposition is a law-statement? Is it just one more empirical proposition (synthetic in its design, contingent in its meaning, and *a posteriori* in its relation to experience)? Or is a law of nature expressed by way of a tautology (analytic in its design, necessary in its meaning, and *a priori* in its relation to experience)? The history of discussions of laws consists either in attempts to analyze them as if they were no more than empirical generalizations, or as if they were but definitions. Some philosophers, dissatisfied with either of these accounts, have undertaken to find some third, more realistic, analysis of laws of nature.

'Dust-bowl empiricists' seem unanimous in viewing laws as being nothing more than generalizations. In this frame of mind $F = ma$ emerges as synthetic, and *a posteriori*. Even empiricists of a sophistication somewhat beyond the dust bowl may press for a similar analysis. Thus Ernst Mach, Bertrand Russell, and C. D. Broad—all construed $F = ma$ as a generalized and highly abstract descriptive account of experiences we have while pushing Steinways and lifting leaden weights. The inclination to treat other classical laws of motion similarly has been manifest in many thinkers, not all of whom have been philosophers. Statisticians, sociologists, and subtle laboratory men often join hands around *laws* and *generalizations,* pronouncing them to be essentially the same.

There are difficulties with such an interpretation. A law like 'All unsupported bodies in terrestrial space move towards center of the earth' is *not* such that we can easily entertain its negation; the conception of a *genuinely* 'levitating' terrestrial body makes the mind boggle. Whereas an exception to a mere generalization like 'All white, blue-eyed tomcats are deaf' does not have such conceptual consequences. If curled up before you now there purrs a white, male, blue-eyed feline—one which possessed a perfect sense of hearing—you would not suddenly have doubts concerning the meaning of 'cat', or of the other words in the generalization. But if this book lifts up off your hands and 'floats', there might be some question in your mind concerning whether you had heretofore understood what *bodies* were and what their 'normal' behavior was really like. In short, genuine laws of nature, although they have a logical form identical to that of generalizations, i.e., $(x) f_x \rightarrow g_x$, nonetheless exert a 'conceptual grip' on the elements of experience—a grip often absent in an actuarial regularity. The mere fact that x and y have always occurred together provides no reason for thinking of x as a 'y-ish'; x and y as related inside a theoretical framework, however, 'hooked together' within what we know, may have just this effect on us. In terrestrial space, unsupported bodies *are* 'freely falling' kinds of things. Classical mechanics provides a conceptual structure in terms of which that relationship is articulated. The theory 'makes' the relationship intelligible, or at least captures whatever it is in the relationship which can be made intelligible. *In fact* all unsupported bodies do (as a matter of actuarial generalization) move toward the center of the earth! This fact makes *sense* only when appreciated as an instantiation of that theory of classical mechanics.

Granted, in a different world our laws of nature might be quite different. But it remains that treating such universal claims as *mere* empirical propositions gives no glimmering of the function of law-statements—to wit, that they interrelate conceptions in a semantically most intimate way.

Other thinkers, less impressed with the context-dependent, synthetic aspects of law-statements, and more taken with their relative indefeasibility, view them as being closer to tautology than do the philosophers mentioned above. Poincaré, Vaihinger, Kolin, and Bullard are philosopher-scientists, who have characterized Newton's laws of motion as being 'mere definitions'. Nothing can count against them because they *define* the relationship between a theory and all its possible subject matters. Thus the laws of ideal fluids generate a theory of fluid mechanics which (since there are *no* ideal fluids) can perhaps be applied to greater or lesser degree to actual fluids in specific states. What a given real fluid does or does not do is thus irrelevant to the design and conception of such a theory. Of particularly recalcitrant fluids, all one can say is that the definitions within such a theory do not make its 'application' to such a subject matter a genuine possibility. Whatever the ultimate account of such a fluid may be, *that* theory cannot supply it. Its boundary conditions just do not provide the links and hooks for grappling liquescent phenomena of that type. All laws of nature may be said to be like this, in principle; that is the position being espoused here. Since it is at the level of its laws that a subject matter *identifies* itself as being suitable for description *via* a given theory, nothing that ever happens within that subject matter could possibly refute such laws. Just as nothing weighed in the pans of a beam-balance can ever upset Archimedes' law of the lever (since the latter is built into the very construction of a beam-balance), and just as nothing weighed by a spring-balance can ever refute Hooke's law (since that law is 'enshrined' in the construction of the spring-balance), so with all laws of nature. They are 'built into' the instruments that do the measuring, into the theories that interpret the measurements, and thus determine which subject matters will, or will not, be managed in accordance with a particular theory. Hence, nothing actually observed or experienced could possibly count against such a law of nature. (Could the actual gait of the Bishop Berkeley ever have refuted the chess rule: ''All Bishops move diagonally to the edge of the board''?)

There is something illuminating about this characterization of laws of nature as being somewhat like definitions, or even like tautologies. It underscores their 'invulnerability', at least so far as the theory of which they are integral parts is applicable to a subject matter at all. It italicizes how laws shape our conceptions of given phenomena by dovetailing particular theories to those phenomena, more or less. Still, it is hard to go 'all the way' with this conception. Statements of laws of nature are synthetic. Their negations entail nothing of the form *Q-and-not-Q*. Even a law like that concerning the *impossi-*

bility of a perpetual motion machine (first kind) is such that its negation, although conceptually untenable to an advanced degree, is not inconsistent in its sign-design. It *must* be factually false for a scientist to claim that he has built a perpetual motion machine. But his claim will not itself contain a contradictory symbol-structure, nor entail such. This being so—i.e., it being clear that law-statements are synthetic—their functions as definitions, stipulations, and 'subject-shapers' is not at all clear, philosophically. Better perhaps to allow that law-statements are formally synthetic, that their negations are not logically inconsistent, and even to grant that there is something descriptively important in their function. All this can be conceded while yet insisting that, within a given scientific theory, a law-statement may be so much built into the 'rules of the game' as to be virtually invulnerable so long as one continues to use that theory (i.e., 'play that game').

Recognizing this latter, that laws of nature are 'invulnerable within the theory they serve to structure', inclines some philosophers to dub them '*necessary* within special scientific languages'. Thus $F = G (m_1 m_2)/r^2$ is 'necessary' (i.e., invulnerable) within every part of classical celestial mechanics. It is inconceivably difficult to think of phenomena such that the general understanding of them proceeds by way of classical mechanics, but with respect to which the law of universal gravitation does not obtain. This, then, is 'provisional necessity', 'relative necessity'— sometimes misleadingly referred to as the 'functionally *a priori'*. $F = G (m_1 m_2)/r^2$ thus functions within classical celestial mechanics *as if* it were a necessary claim.

Concerning the *a posteriority* of laws, this again is beyond serious dispute. In a different universe, our laws of nature could be other than they are. (Kant once entertained the possibility that our world might have been constituted according to an inverse threefold ratio $[F = G (m_1 m_2)/r^3]$, rather than the inverse square—a possibility in every way self-consistent and meaningful. The most one can say of such suggestion is that it is empirically false of our world as it *is* constituted, which clearly marks the *a posteriority* of the law in question.)

Thus laws are such that their statements are (1) synthetic in sign-design, (2) 'necessary' within the theory which they help to constitute, and (3) *a posteriori* with respect to their epistemological status. Are they then both 'synthetic and necessary' [*à la* (1) and (2)·]? Yes, if it is *relative* necessity, and not absolute necessity, which is understood. Some synthetic claims (*L*) are virtually invulnerable within the descriptive statement-systems of which they are part.

The quest for a synthetic *a priori*—a quest central to much of the history of modern philosophy—strikes this author as being confused in several ways. Granted, it was Hume's unacceptable analysis of Newton's laws of motion (as 'statistical regularities plus psychological expectations') that awakened Kant from his "dogmatic slumbers". The specifically Kantian resolution, however, seems somehow

conceptually unsound today. That law-statements
are synthetic (they have consistent negations)—and
are yet invulnerable within the languages they help
to shape—provides no occasion for any illicit philosophical 'mixing' of logical alternatives which are
sharply distinct. Both Broad and Peierls conclude
that, since law-statements have both *synthetic* and
necessary elements, they must therefore be 'mix-
tures' of these constituents. But the 'unmixability'
of oil and water is as nothing when compared to the
'unmixability' of the *synthetic* and the absolutely
necessary.

A further feature of law-statements lends to this
confusing picture of 'mixing the unmixable'. Law-
statements are expressed in sentences. *Which* statement a given law-sentence does express will itself
be a context-dependent matter.

Thus *'Le ciel est bleu'* and 'The sky is blue' are
two sentences that make the same assertion: the sky
is blue. Two sentences, one claim. On the other hand,
the sentence 'The sun rises in the east' may express
either an empirical truth, or a tautology. If 'east'
is the name of that place where the sun rises (wher-
ever that may be), then, even should tomorrow's
dawn be in the direction of Antarctica—the sun must
still be rising in the east. But if 'east' is determined
by an appeal to celestial coordinates rather than by
definition, then it will be a contingent matter that
the sun, on any given day, does rise in the east. One
sentence, two claims. Law-sentences derive their
maddening versatility from this same context de-
pendence. The uses to which the sentence '$F = ma$'

can be put are wide ranging enough to determine
law-statements of almost any location on the ana-
lytic-synthetic spectrum. (See N. R. Hanson, *Patterns of Discovery,* ch. V.)

Hypothetico-Deduction

So much for the 'overview' of theories; we have
spoken of what they are, what they do, and how they
relate to some wider philosophical issues. This still
leaves the conceptual analysis of the 'fine structure'
of theories largely undiscussed; how are they constituted, what distinguishes their logical structure,
what is their 'grammar'? One significant response
here consists in characterizing theories as 'hypothetico-deductive systems'. On this view, scientific
theories are first and foremost systems of inference,
within which every component proposition is located
either at the 'bottom of the page' of inquiry (where
the propositions resemble theorems in purely deductive systems), or else it falls 'mid-page'—'beneath' claims of greater generality, and 'above'
claims of less generality. Or, finally, propositions
within a theory may be of the very highest level,
the 'from which' everything else in the system inferentially follows. Still, these highest-order claims are
not just posited, or assumed, or presupposed simply
for the purpose of deducing everything below—as
in a deductive theory. Rather, on the hypothetico-
deductive view, even such highest order claims are
themselves ultimately empirical in nature. They are
a posteriori, factually true, or factually false, even

though determination of this may require subtle techniques of analysis.

There may be some question concerning whether scientific theories are systems of 'propositions' at all! An intratheoretic expression like '$F = G (m_1 m_2) / r^2$' is a propositional schema—and as such it is neither true nor false. Such a symbol-cluster can express a proposition only when observational values are inserted for the variable terms, or when the entire expression is universally quantified. Such quantification is often tacitly assumed, within the boundaries set by particular languages. Thus the law of universal gravitation usually begins "For any bodies whatever . . ." But note that the business of rendering a symbol-network into being a 'system of propositions' requires explicit attention somewhere (1) in the correspondence rules, or (2) in the 'coordinating definitions', or (3) in the abstract interpretations which transform the 'symbology' of a theory into something semantically intelligible.

Within this thought-framework scientific theories are much like isolated symbolic games, whose properties are determined by formal 'algorithmic' considerations. Such a theory can effect contact with its subject matter only 'at the bottom of the page', where one finds expressions which, when suitably linked to the 'outside world' via coordinating definitions and correspondence rules, will generate observation statements. These latter will be certifiably true or false (certifiable by observation). The measure of a theory's empirical utility, then, will be the degree to which these observation statements turn out to be true, rather than false. Should the verdict go toward recognizing a given theory's predictions as true far more often than as false, this will tend, indirectly, to confirm the theory as a whole. To the extent that this happens, all the laws within the theory—i.e., all the high-order hypotheses—will, insofar, also be confirmed.

This position has a great deal going for it. Worthies like Hempel, Braithwaite, Popper, Carnap, and J. S. Mill, by articulating variations of this hypothetico-deductive analysis, have succeeded well in accounting for some aspects of scientific theories. The 'all-or-nothing' feature of our acceptance of most theories at once becomes clear. One cannot decompose an inferential system piecemeal, preserving just those components in it which have been favored in experience. A deductive system (and a hypothetico-deductive system also) stands or falls *en bloc.* When experience fails to support its consequences, to that extent the entire theory has been revealed as vulnerable—marked as possibly untrustworthy within all further inquiries. One solid body observed floating in mid-air, supported by *nothing,* will send all of classical mechanics to the bottom. The hypothetico-deductive account of theories illuminates this point as well as, or better than, alternative analyses.

That account also demarcates what we understand by an *anomaly.* Within an established theory our 'expectations' of a given subject matter can be exfoliated with deductive precision. 'Normal expectations' are identical with a hypothetico-deductive exposition of our knowledge. Anomalies, then, are those happenings whose descriptions express the *negation* of observation statements entailed within a hypothetico-deductive 'unpacking' of some well-established theory. Thus, it was expected that the emission of radiation would always be a continuous process; we expected Sirius to move rectilinearly in its translation across the stellar background—not to 'wiggle'; we anticipated that Uranus would 'keep time' in its orbit like all other then-known (pre-1846) Newtonian objects. When such 'theoretical expectations' are not fulfilled, the resulting situation is said to be 'anomalous', as were the undulations of Sirius and the decelerations and accelerations of Uranus. Indeed, most features of the anatomy of theories receive a clear elucidation within hypothetico-deductive accounts.

Retroduction

To what extent, however, does such a position enable us to understand the dynamics of 'theory construction'? How are the rational strategies of scientific problem-solving illuminated by works such as those of Braithwaite and Reichenbach? The latter duo will quickly remark that they are not concerned with the 'process of discovery'. Matters of sociology, psychology, and inspired intuition are of no interest to the thinker for whom 'rational reconstruction' and 'axiomatization' are primary objectives. It thus appears to 'hypothetico-deductive' philosophers that any analysis, such as that of Peirce, which passes under the name of 'retroduction', must be irrelevant to conceptual analysis. Retroduction *must* concern itself, apparently, with mere matters of fact, with sundry issues of psychology, with sociological and historical considerations having much to do with the *process,* the 'psycho-dynamics', of problem-solving, but little, if anything, to do with comprehending the conceptual structure thereof.

There are reasons for resisting such a final and uncompromising appraisal of retroduction. Aristotle (*Posterior Analytics,* II, 19), and Peirce himself (*Collective Papers,* I), certainly knew the differences between matters of fact and matters of analysis. It misrepresents the positions of these thinkers to suggest, that, when writing about science, they concerned themselves only with the former. They took themselves to be doing philosophy. They *were* doing philosophy!

Granted, they were not (*à la* Braithwaite and Reichenbach) undertaking *ex post facto* logical reconstructions of the 'argument-anatomy' of Finished Research Reports. But it does not follow that they were hence exclusively concerned with psychology. The exhaustive and exclusive dichotomy 'Psychology or Logic?' may win debates occasionally, but it cannot win the guerdon of truth. Many features of the actual problem solving of ordinary people, and of ordinary scientists, require understanding the *criteria* in virtue of which one can distinguish *good* reasons from *bad* reasons. Long before an investigator has finished his inquiry, has solved his problem, and has finally written up his research report, there must have been many occasions when he found himself forced to use his head, to invoke his reason, and to decide between those speculations which seemed potentially fruitful, and those which did not. There are such things as 'proto-hypotheses'; these test our capacity to delineate *ranges* of plausible conjectures within which we would be prepared to argue that our final solution is most likely to lie. Determining these ranges of possibility and plausibility will often be based on reasoning of a fairly exacting variety. Thus, while still an undergraduate (and long before he succeeded in fashioning the final form of the law of universal gravitation), Newton reasoned that the law, whatever its ultimately divined form, would certainly be of inverse square structure. His reasoning was trenchant, resting upon the deductive linkages between Kepler's third law $[T^2 \propto r^3]$ and Huygen's law of centrifugal and centripetal force $[F \propto r/T^2]$. From these it follows that *if* the sun exerts a centripetal force upon the planets, then that F will be proportional to r/r^3, or $1/r^2$. Newton had good reasons for anticipating that the Law would be of that certain *kind*. His reasons then (1661–1665) appear to us even today to be good reasons. Yet such cerebrations obtained twenty years before any final formulation of the law in question.

Regarding the functioning of theories within technical science, the hypothetico-deductive account seems illuminating vis-à-vis our ideas of hypothesis-testing, and terse expositions of the results of that testing. The retroductive emphasis, however, is more centered upon the conceptual aspects of problem-solving. The primary datum within the latter is the *anomaly* itself—the perplexing occasion for further inquiry. The leading consideration within hypothetico-deductive thinking is the well-formed exposition of the problem's *solution*. This is in answer to the question "What follows from these premisses (i.e., hypotheses, laws and initial conditions)?" The leading question in retroductive thinking is "From what premisses can this anomaly be shown to follow?"

Can one solve problems *reasonably* within scientific inquiry? Of course. To that extent there are canons of reason, criteria of rationality, which distinguish good technique from bad, promising conjectures from dubious ones, likely directions of inquiry from unpromising courses of research. Such criteria, or strategies, might well be examined by philosophers of science in terms which do not 'reduce' to being mere psychological speculation. Aristotle, Mill, Whewell, Peirce, Toulmin, and Hanson may have made some faltering starts along this path of inquiry. But, faltering or not, such a philosophical interest is to be distinguished, on the one hand, from the 'formalizing' tendencies of Axiomatizers within the hypothetico-deductive 'school', and, on the other hand, from the psychological patter of scientific biographers concerned with the thought processes and psychological conditioning of discoverers. Examining the rational strategies of scientific problem-solving, therefore, does not collapse into being logical reconstruction or psycho-factual recitation. It is, in principle, philosophical inquiry, of a different kind. There are too many important events within history of science that are philosophically deformed by treatments guided solely via hypothetico-deductive formal structure of finished research reports. The discovery of Sirius' companion, of Neptune, of the neutrino, the positron, etc.—these were disclosures responding to perplexing, anomalous situations, deviation from the expected. Such discoveries often result from positing (or 'divining') theoretical entities in the course of 'putting anomalies to sleep.' This epistemological point is lost while philosophers shuffle to provide elegant, formally economical presentations of the support for claims that such entities as the neutrino and Neptune actually *exist;* this in addition to the earlier reflections that *if* they did exist, then some specific anomaly would be thereby resolved. What is called "The Astronomy of the Invisible" is a continuing instantiation of this point (See "Sirius" in the *Encyclopaedia Britannica.*) Perceiving that *if* some such things as Sirius' companion and Neptune did exist our observational perplexities would evaporate —*this* is neither a formal argument in support of the *de facto* existence of trans-*observabilia,* nor is it a subtle sampling of the intracranial processes of discoverers. Many significant solutions to scientific problems have been generated via rationally directed appeals to 'as if' entities, theoretical entities, the intellectual need for which has provided practical occasion for experimentalists to seek after such *denotata* within the subject matter.

Theoretical Entities

'One cannot give a mechanical explanation of the very things that make mechanical explanation possible.' This sentiment is natural for the thinker who puzzles over the epistemological and semantical status of *denotata* such as force-free bodies, rigid levers, frictionless surfaces, ideal fluids, etc. One can provide mechanical explanations of actual, observable phenomena—the trajectories of hockey pucks, the steering linkage in automobiles, billiard balls on felt-covered slate tables, the properties of cold air and hot oil—by anchoring descriptions of such familiar objects and processes to inferential networks which hook up with what is calculated to happen in 'the pure case'. Knowing how objects would move through an ideal fluid is what allows us to calculate the actual behavior of non-ideal objects (e.g., aircraft) through non-ideal fluids (e.g., the air above us). So the very comprehension of everyday processes and laboratory events depends on conceptual extrapolations to what would obtain with 'pure designata' released-in-thought from the 'imperfections' of their empirical embodiment (another droplet of Aristotelian metaphor which generates seas of philosophical punch).

Full scientific understanding then, may require such arguments from 'the pure case', these latter resting in references to theoretical entities. Some philosophers, of course, will deny the essential irreducibility of such theoretical references. They will decompose the latter into their 'observational' components, and other components the precise appraisal of which will depend upon the philosophical objectives of the appraiser.

Craig's Theorem

Consider any scientific statement whatever—e.g., "The transverse magnetic field deflected the beta-particles." It might be argued that every such claim could be restated, without any loss of 'operational' meaning, in strictly nontheoretical, observational form. The only way we can even ascertain the existence of a magnet field is to shoot a 'test particle' through it, recording the resultant deflections to the particle's original trajectory. The only way we can ascertain the existence of a beta-particle is to note the molar-observable 'footprints' it leaves (e.g., in a cloud or bubble chamber, or in an emulsion). Hence a strictly operational equivalent of the statement above would concern the observable deflection-curves traced by water droplets formed on ionized gas particles, or traced by bubbles in a supercooled fluid; it would record thus the 'electron' path's sense of curvature and the degree to which that track is to be distinguished from others noted on various occasions in the past; and it will cite the conditions of experimentation which were operative on all relevant occasions, past and present. The resulting paraphrase would, of course, be very long indeed— possibly interminable. But it would have the philosophical 'virtue' of excluding all theoretical entities, whose properties surpass the information gained via such observational encounters in the laboratory.

The message?: every operationally sound scientific sentence will, sooner or later, be statable in observationally responsible terms.

What if some component of a scientific sentence is not completely capturable within such a corresponding operational translation? Then that term may have had no business being within a proper scientific language at all; it may not be 'operationally meaningful'. At the very least, such a term must be segregated from all those other terms in a science which do pass the 'operational' test. The explanation of such a term may turn on 'metaphysical' or 'psychological' considerations.

But what of science itself! The Craig theorem is to the effect that every scientific theory can be cleft atwain—into two sets of sentences. In the one set will be all those sentences which contain no theoretical terms at all. They will be operationally respectable. The other set will contain all other terms, whose appraisal will hinge on multiform considerations. And these will be all the sentences in the theory. This harmless representation seems to be all that Craig had in mind—that the observationally tractable part of a theory could be represented as a conjunction of all its constituent observation-sentences. Some philosophers of science have carried Craig's message much further. They have construed the theorem as claiming, *à la* our earlier remarks about 'operational translations', that *only* the conjunction of a theory's observation-sentences has a rightful place in the scientists' attention. Everything respectable within science itself can therefore be conveyed in operationally significant terms (is this a tautology?), and the appropriate semantical vehicle for this is the string of observation-statements generable therefrom—the possibility of generating which for the entire theory, without remainder, is the main test of a theory's 'operational respectability' and the main burden of this extreme construal of the Craig theorem, a construal which surely exceeds the original intentions of Professor Craig himself.

The inspiration, and motivation, behind this extremism is clear. The 'formal' lineage is obvious. (So is the dead horse of radical empiricism.) Any continuous function F is representable as the complete series (usually infinite) of all those n-tuple terms which comprise membership of the expanded series over which F ranges. Analytically there is no more to F than what can be represented thus. So, also, it may seem to some philosophers that there is no more to any theoretically impregnated scientific statement than the observation-sentence 'unpacking' which sets out in a linear semantical sequence all the meanings 'confusedly' compressed within the statement itself.

On then to the next level of abstraction: Every scientific theory (usually an algebraic network of terms functionally related) is representable as the infinite conjunction of all its constituent observation-sentences. This is the radical and extreme extension of Craig's theorem, which was originally a pronouncement of much more modest scope.

By this extended account there is no function for a theoretical term (like 'electron', 'force', 'psi', etc.) beyond what can be unpacked from it at the most uncomplicated level of observation-statement. Anything in excess of this is 'metaphysical embroidery' or perhaps a 'heuristic carrot' to be held before the scientist's nose. In a sophisticated and uncompromising form, this position has obvious similarities to the older and newer positivisms, empiricisms, and operationalisms. Is there any way of questioning such an analysis without at the same time collapsing spinelessly into a soft idealism, or becoming a Rococo Kantian—or (even worse) a navel-contemplatory Aristotelian?

One *could* consider the intratheoretic roles of theoretical terms, bypassing the ontological and operational issues thereby. It just isn't true that after having remarked all the extrasystematic correlations of a term like *e* with *observabilia* (e.g., pointer-readings, titration-colors, deflection-measures), one has said everything about the intrasystematic functioning of such terms. Indeed with this much only at hand, one has said *nothing* about the latter. Reflect upon the largely uninterpreted term 'straight line' within pure Euclidean geometry; its functions there are in no way illuminated by our considerable conversations concerning correspondence rules and coordinating definitions, in virtue of which 'straight line' is observationally strapped to things like rays of light, taut strings, or the surfaces of optically flat glass (when viewed on edge). No attempt to set out the reduction-sentence equivalent of geometrical optics can indicate how 'straight line' helps the inference-nets which structure optical theories to operate as they do.

There may be many intrasystematic functions of theoretical terms which are not collapsible into conjoint references to observational experiences. Nor, on the other hand, are they representable as being but symbolic shorthand (i.e., substitution rules making some short expression like '4' or 'Σ' equivalent to several longer, operationally transparent expressions). Indeed, to the extent that a *systematic* exposition of a subject matter is involved in 'understanding' it, to that same degree theoretical terms help us to comprehend phenomena; they function so as to systematize and structure observation-sentence clusters within a discipline.

How then does one determine whether a statement, one which irreducibly includes a theoretical term, is *true* or *false?* How does the thesis of verification bear upon our appreciation of these diversities of discourse within science?

Verification

The 'verification-meaning controversy' of the thirties was at once a cause of, and an effect of, philosophical concern about the nature of science. Once one has made observability a virtual criterion of the legitimacy of scientific discourse, it is but a small step to argue that any unit of discourse will count as descriptively significant only to the extent that it 'deals with' observables—only to the degree to which one can have a clear idea of what such discourse describes, what state of affairs it seeks to delineate. A scientific statement is meaningful to us only insofar as we can specify what kind of observations would disclose it as certifiably true. It is at the heart of reduction-sentence translation that terms which are in no way correlatable with observables, and statements which (because they include such terms) are not decisively testable by way of experience— that such terms, and such statements, are just not semantically well formed. They are deficient in descriptive meaning. Psychology, and tradition to the contrary notwithstanding, such discourse is not 'scientifically meaningful'. Thus, the verification principle.

The principle generated conversation, consternation, and considerable confusion. It encouraged an 'antitheoretical' development within the sciences, and within philosophical and historical commentaries about science. 'Dust-bowl empiricism', as found amongst Questionnaire-designing Sociologists, Rat-running Psychologists, Species-counting Biologists, Substance-analyzing Chemists and Datagathering Physicists—is not too far removed from the radical philosophy of verification. Intense concern with techniques of corroboration, with success in prediction, and maximizing accuracy within the statistical gathering of data—all this has often led to de-emphasis on explaining and understanding perplexities. It might be urged that success in prediction, and the understanding of a subject matter, are one and the same; but that is a question *for* philosophical discussion, not a sergeant-major's command preparatory to all discussion.

The issue here centers on a perhaps too-restricted conception of what verifying a claim, or a theory, actually consists in. [A philosophical position, extended beyond a concern with single propositions to a study of *systems* of propositions (i.e., theories), can sometimes be broadening and comprehensive.] Might it not be the case then that, in addition to observational felicity, predictive power, and success in confirmation, one should also consider how far *understanding* is conveyed via a proposition-system? Ptolemaic astronomy and Copernican astronomy were, during the latter half of the sixteenth century, on a par vis-à-vis success and confirmation. At that moment in history observation could not decide between these two statement-networks. This alone, however, was insufficient to prevent some thinkers from regarding the latter as 'verified' and the former as not so—it being clear that such thinkers packed the meaning "provides us with an instrument for *understanding* phenomena" into the expression 'is verified'. Too often "is successful in observation and prediction" is all that is allowed to serve as the semantical content of 'is verified'.

Such a broadening being granted *pro tem*, we can perceive again our contrast between Scylloid and Charybdoid philosophical postures; where verification is restricted to corroboration-in-terms-of-sense-experience, one result is a distrust of all theoretical science and, indeed, of all statements of fact which transcend the lowest order of our perceptual encounters. 'Dust-bowl empiricists' thus seem indifferently hostile toward astrologists, cosmologists, and sociologists. But, surely, to the degree that sociologists and cosmologists, by their special theories and techniques of inquiry, can explain perplexing aspects of their intricate subject matters, and can render intelligible what might otherwise have been a chaotic confusion of conceptual concerns—to that degree such disciplines will justifiably be said to be verified. So the *via media* here lies this side of the dust bowl; phenomenalistic sense-encounters are not the answer to the question "How can scientific inquiry both explain, and yet remain responsible to observation and experience?"

Falsification

There is no reason for letting our verdict oscillate to the other extreme, however. Another reason why it can be misleading to rivet attention exclusively to matters of verification is that this criterion allows disciplines like astrology, graphology, and phrenology, all to pass as responsible and respectable. These 'sciences' experience no difficulty in indicating *ex post facto* events which were vaguely forecast by the practitioners thereof. (Compare the contemporary best-seller.) How many astrologers did, after the fact, proudly refer back to their horoscopes of 1930, mysterious scribblings which foretold great changes being brought about by a dark man of erratic temperament? Hitler was seen by them all as the fulfillment of their prophecy. But such unfocused hunches were not predictions. They were never respectable components within genuine scientific theories. Because it would not have been possible, at the time of their first enunciation, to specify in detail *then* what would count as evidence *against* such claims. Even knowing what is meant by a prediction requires being able to articulate in advance what events, were they to take place, would falsify that prediction. All too often the forecasts of astrologers, graphologists, and phrenologists seem compatible with anything whatever. Occasionally this same verdict has been applied to theories inside ostensibly 'proper science', e.g., those of Velikowsky, Lycenko, Miller, Ehrenhaft, Spencer, Priestley, Stahl, and Hooke. But insofar as the meaning of scientific terms is to connect with operations and observations, *falsification* is no less essential than *verification* as a criterion of acceptability. The great theories of yesterday have indeed been verified; but we know what it would have been like to falsify them. Therein lies their semantical strength. The former, verification, in the absence of the latter, falsifiability, is not a reliable guide to the achievements of science.

Models

Akin to these considerations is the scientific model, about which so much has been written during the recent past. The conceptual structure displayed via the articulation of a model—such as the Saturn-model of the hydrogen atom, the shell-model of the atomic nucleus, the telephone switchboard-model of the human brain, the hydraulic conduit-model of the neural fibers—that structure suggests a possible idea-framework for otherwise unstructured ensembles of descriptions. Such frameworks of ideas hook the descriptions together with inferential links. The model which suggests these inferential linkages between statements fosters intelligibility; it aids in our understanding of a subject matter; it provides channels of interconnexity between states of affairs which (except for these links) might remain conceptually isolated and independent of each other. Explaining perplexities requires linking them to the normal cases—the unperplexing. The unusual becomes unsurprising only when inferentially hooked to the usual. Models suggest to us ranges of possible explanations—routes to the unsurprising. Knowledge may begin in astonishment, as Aristotle observed, but it surely doesn't end there. Full knowledge of anything consists in expecting every feature of that thing "as a matter of course."

But saying what models *do* does not indicate how differently different models may function. Nor does it suggest how with every model there may be disadvantages as well as virtues. Since it is an objective of every model to provide an inference-structure for propositions descriptive of a subject matter—a structure which is neither simple nor perspicuous within the descriptions themselves (else why would a model be needed in explaining them?)—it follows that the structure must be presented in a *different* way through the model from what obtains within the subject matter itself. To the extent that one appreciates the model's structure as superimposed on the data, without also swallowing the differences (without, that is, investing the subject matter with features unique to the model only, and foreign to the former), to that extent the model is serving well. Still, the scientist who uses models in his reflections must always remain alert to the possibility that his questions are inspired only by properties of the model, having nothing directly to do with the subject matter itself. Thus the water-closet model of animal instinct, as invoked by Niko Tinbergen, helped us understand the 'all-or-nothing' response of instinctive impulse once the 'cistern chain handle' had been pulled. Instinctive behavior 'flows' all at once when the pipes are opened (to use another model). But Tinbergen was at once on the hunt for 'leaks in the instinctual conduitry', 'blockages', 'displacements', etc. Some of these were suggestive and helpful. Others not at all. Again, is the area of electronic influence around the nucleus of the hydrogen atom in any way like the rings of Saturn? To a Nagoaka, or a Rutherford, the suggestion was attention consuming. But the question is now seldom asked.

Thus a model, persuasively to present an idea-structure as a possible linkage-format for descriptions of a given subject matter, *must* differ from the subject matter. If it were not different, the original structure would itself be observationally obvious to everyone who confronted the descriptions, or at least as obvious as in the model. Either that or it would be obvious to no one, not even the would-be model-builder. Models are thus a way of presenting structures that might *possibly* inforce subject matters. They do so in ways psychologically more compelling (i.e., simpler and more focused) than would just another confrontation with the subject matter itself.

Suppose one undertook to minimize, indeed eliminate, the differences between the model and the original phenomena. Scientists have felt that whenever it is necessary to articulate a structure (the model's) in terms different from those directly applicable to the subject matter itself, this constitutes an imperfection in the 'state of the art' at that time. The Saturnian model, the Shell model, the two-fluid model—all were advanced as expositional ploys, always with the embarrassed reassurance that more knowledge of the subject matter would render the model unnecessary. A hypothetical objective of science then, might be, systematically and surely to minimize the area of divergence and disparity between the original phenomena and the theoretical model. Ultimately science will articulate 'what's what' of phenomena, *sans* models and all other toys.

Thus the 5-inch balsa wood model of a Spitfire airplane is 'less faithful' to the original than a 15-inch metal-covered, flying model, one with movable controls. Both of these are 'less faithful' to the real thing than would be a construction half the size of the original machine, a model possessed of *every* structural component within the actual Spitfire. Even this last disparity (i.e., being half-size) might be eliminated in a model faithful to the original in *every* way. The result, however, would not be a *model* of a Spitfire; it would *be* the production of

another operational Spitfire! Whatever might have
been one's motivation to have a model of the original, it would still remain unfulfilled if the result was
'only' another original! (Harvey didn't puzzle out
the circulation of the blood just by becoming a
father—thereby helping to bring another circulatory
system into existence. Reproducing perplexities ex-
actly is not the same as highlighting their structures.)

Therefore, by completely eliminating *all* differences between the model and the original state of
affairs one ends up destroying the very thing the
model was meant to achieve—namely, the provision
of an 'awareness of structure' absent from the original confrontation with a complex of phenomena. [Of
course, if the full-size Spitfire reproduction was
amplified with display circuitry which illuminated
the fuel system in green lights when one pressed a
certain button, or the ignition system in red lights,
or the hydraulic system in blue lights—this would
again have become a model. It would be reinstated
as a model because, by such differences from the
original, aspects of the latter would now stand out
in a way unrealized in any mere replication, however
faithful it may be to the facts. This is itself a clue
to one of the main differences between laws of nature
and statistical generalizations. Although both have
the form (x) $(fx \rightarrow gx)$, the generalization is just a
descriptive replication of *observabilia;* the law is
never just that. And a single sentence of the form
(x) $(fx \rightarrow gx)$ may *now* express a law, and at another
time express a mere generalization—depending on

whether the context of its employment is one within which our attention is directed to a recitation of data, or to the form of those data, Kepler's third law, $T^2 \propto r^3$, has had both kinds of uses.]

What models must do to *be* models is related to what theories must do to *be* theories, and related also to what sciences must do in order to *be* sciences. Understanding perplexing phenomena requires attending to what "makes them go." Within the staggering variety of ways of directing attention to special features of complex subject matters, one thing is common to them all; there must always be *some* differences between (1) the mode of presentation, or the representation (i.e., the model, the theory, the science), and (2) the big, blooming, confusing, phenomenal perplexities which drove men to try to understand them all in the first place. Detailed photographs of jumbled jigsaw puzzles are just as puzzling as what was photographed; they are not different *enough*.

At one end of this philosophical world there will always be those for whom differences between the mode of representation and the properties of the original phenomena (assuming such differences to be articulable at all) will always constitute a blemish, an imperfection, an unwarranted heuristic prop —or even a metaphysical excrescence—upon the primary business of 'telling the truth' in science. Such thinkers will recoil from 'larger pictures' of phenomenon, toward ever-refined descriptive techniques, toward more precise laboratory equipment, toward descriptions which are increasingly close to the reports of sense experience. Depending upon how far the philosopher of science is prepared to move along this spectral world line, he can be located somewhere with the empiricists, or the positivists, or the experimentalists, or the observationalists, or the operationalists—all of them possible, valuable philosophies of science. All such philosophers, like Raphael's depiction of Aristotle in *The School of Athens*, 'point downward', to the foundation of experience. To the extent that the scholar stresses 'the bigger picture'—even at the possible risk of doing fleeting injustice to experience—to that extent he will, like Raphael's Plato, 'point upwards'; he may even end up saying, with Hegel, "so much the worse for the facts." This is an extreme position rarely to be found within responsible philosophy of science. But there are surely occasions when, while reading Whewell, Meyerson, Poincaré, Cassirer, Natorp, Cohen, Blanshard, and Capek, one is almost prepared to encounter just such extremities. But, somewhere short of that 'far-out' pole, one can locate conceptual coordinates occupied by philosophers of all persuasions who are unready to allow theory, thought, hypothesis, and experiment to be reduced to 'nothing more than' a congeries of wide-eyed encounters with the phenomena of this world. The scientific encounter, say such philosophers, is more than a scratching amongst the data of experience, yet never so much more as to become indistinguishable from artistic or even mystical experience.

Our objective in everything that has gone before has been to locate these polar-types of philosopher as they wander through ranges of connected subjects within philosophy of science. In each foray *our* search has been for some nonextreme 'middle way' —some resolution sensitive both to the existence of our Scylla and of our Charybdis—but sensitive also to the practices of respected scientists, and to the best analyses of responsible philosophers. It was hoped that a kind of conceptual chart might have been set out, a map representing many of the problems perennial within philosophy of science. Perhaps this 'Baedeker tour' which we have sketched in dotted lines—a journey which moves (conservatively) between the prominences so dear to idea-cartographers—may seem mild and unimaginative to the reader. (This verdict is usually passed on tours as conceived by Baedeker, AAA, and American Express.) But even so, the route might be sufficiently well marked and annotated to provide occasions for adventurous digressions off the beaten path, into untrod and unrowed regions of philosophical inquiry, the traversal of which may be made more exciting by the proximity of Scylla and Charybdis.